MODERN
TURKISH
ARCHITECTURE

MODERN TURKISH ARCHITECTURE

Edited by

Renata Holod and
Ahmet Evin

University of Pennsylvania Press

Library of Congress Cataloging in Publication Data
Main entry under title:

Modern Turkish architecture.

    Includes bibliographical references and index.
    1. Architecture, Modern—20th century—Turkey—
Addresses, essays, lectures. 2. Architecture—
Turkey—Addresses, essays, lectures. I. Holod, Renata.
II. Evin, Ahmet.
NA1368.M6 1984   722′.5   83-25990
ISBN 0-8122-7925-5

Printed in the United States of America

CONTENTS

PREFACE

In connection with the celebration of the centennial of Mustafa Kemal Atatürk's birth (1881-1981), the University of Pennsylvania, its Middle East Center, and University Museum held a photographic exhibition and seminar on architecture in Turkey from 1923 to 1980. This publication is the outcome of the two events which were held at the end of the centennial year in March 1982. Funding was provided by the special Turkish government centennial funds, through the good offices of the Cultural Ambassador, His Excellency Talât Halman, and by the University of Pennsylvania, with the help of Acting Provost Louis Girifalco and of Dean Robert H. Dyson, Jr., then also Acting Director of the University Museum. Dr. Suha Özkan, Vice-President of the Middle East Technical University, was instrumental in organizing the photographic material and the program of the seminar. Our thanks are due to Professor Cecil Striker, Chairman, History of Art Department and to Professor Thomas Naff, Director, Middle East Center, for moral and logistic support. Salih Memecan and Sibel Dostoğlu were instrumental in preparing the exhibition and the seminar papers. David Underwood aided in editorial tasks. Additional support staff was provided by funds drawn from the Aga Khan Foundation grant to Professor Renata Holod. Illustrations, unless otherwise indicated, were provided by the photographic archives of the Middle East Technical University. Graphic design is by Salih Memecan.

INTRODUCTION

Histories of modern architecture have tended to identify and analyze a single metropolitan tradition. Until recently, they have been almost exclusively concerned with the development of an architectural geneology or of its several intertwined strands. These histories found their examples in a limited number of locations, in Western Europe and the United States, and could be more appropriately called the accounts of works of selected architects rather than comprehensive histories of contemporary world architecture. Indeed, it was probably not the intention of studies in modern architecture to be inclusive or even illustrative. Still, the rest of the world has also built and has, in the last fifty years, transformed itself physically to an even greater extent than the celebrated places of modern architecture. The models used for this transformation have for the most part been derived from the metropolitan tradition or later from the International Style. But all the while there has also existed an alternate search for a regionally based and regionally recognizable idiom in the newly built environment.

This book is the first one in English to trace the development of this new environment, the rise of the architectural profession, and the transformation of the building industry in Turkey from the first decades of this century to the present day. It is also the presentation of a school of thought which has developed among architectural historians, practitioners, and critics and which, although methodologically connected with architectural history at large, has its own internal language, preoccupations and, to some extent, its own criteria.

This collection of essays provides an opportunity to examine the processes which produced the newly built environment and the critical language which has been developed to describe them. In these essays, individual buildings have been evaluated primarily according to their fit into a socio-political context and their response to cultural ideas or ideologies. The overriding concern of the authors can be understood as a search for authenticity of Turkishness, as the latter is continually defined and redefined by political and economic realities, and social and cultural attitudes.

In the first chapter, Ilhan Tekeli outlines the social background and considers the economic factors which affected the development of architecture and of the building industry in Turkey. He relates this development to the emergence and differentiation of the architectural profession. To explain the nature of the profession, he has appropriated the economic concept of a peripheral country in the capitalist world market system and has extended the concept to cultural, intellectual and therefore, architectural spheres. Accordingly, the late Ottoman and early Republican period in architecture is seen as one of high dependency on the

West, which was the source of capital and, as importantly, of technology, ideas and forms. The latter became ingredients Turkish architects reordered to create new styles which they called national. Tekeli proposes that an internally coherent expression in architecture, and culture, can only develop in closed economic systems, such as Turkey's in the 1930s, and that any economic opening, such as lowering of tariffs or eased import restriction will, by necessity, usher an international expression or international styles in architecture. Ultimately, he asks whether architects in peripheral countries are capable of making major contributions to the universe of building and architecture at large or whether they will continue to be constrained by the economic and technological limitations of their peripherality. Conversely, does integration into the world economic system result in a wholesale borrowing of ideas, designs and technology from elsewhere and the obliteration in a country of its own architectural tradition, local forms and culture of building? Are architects conditioned to utilize other building cultures and professional methods to answer increasingly specialized needs? Finally, Tekeli asks under what circumstances the universal and the contemporary can be coupled with the traditional and the vernacular.

The history of modern Turkish architecture provides a rich variety of clues to these questions which are treated implicitly or explicitly by the other contributors to the volume. Yıldırım Yavuz and Suha Özkan, in chapters two and three, discuss the emergence of new building types during the last decades of the Ottoman Empire and the first years of the Republic in terms of individual buildings designed and built by Europeans and European-trained architects. Vedat [Tek] and Kemalettin Bey have been singled out by the authors as the founders of the modern architectural profession in Turkey and, particularly, as the instigators of the search for regional expression in architecture. Afife Batur sees the 1930s as the period during which the forms of Government buildings were developed and coincided with the articulation of the official state ideology. In chapter 4, she documents the rejection of the Modern Movement in architecture in favor of monumental, official architecture of the German and Italian regimes. Batur also chronicles the influences of economic policies, development programs and municipal codes on urban centers as well as on the rural hinterland. Private building activity almost disappeared under the wartime economy of the 1940s, but the Government's building program continued, and buildings commissioned and planned earlier were completed. Üstün Alsaç describes the predominant style of the period, formed partly by what has been called new traditionalism or state-inspired architecture and partly by the search for Turkishness in the Anatolian past. In the following chapter, Mete Tapan discusses the diffusion of the International Style in Turkey beginning with the years following World War II and relates the subsequent changes in the architectural sphere to the economic policies and the pro-Western orientation of the Government. Implied in his argument is that designs developed in a peripheral country are not able to compete in the international market, and that Turkish architects in the 1950s had to follow in the footsteps of their European colleagues who provided them with appropriate models to fulfill the demands for new functions.

Over the last three decades Turkey achieved a high level of economic growth attended by major social and demographic changes and by a building activity of enormous proportions. The control of the architect over the shaping of the built environment has declined in proportion to the growth of the unplanned shanty towns (gecekondu). The architectural profession itself became stratified, with a few practitioners designing prestige buildings and many others taking routine bureaucratic jobs or working as contractors and salesmen. Architects no longer constituted a cohesive group identified closely with political or intellectual leadership. Attilla Yücel in Chapter 7 discusses these changes in the profession since 1960 and traces the evolution of a complex architectural criticism paralleling the history of the profession. Yıldız Sey deals with the history of housing and housing problems in Turkey since the beginning of the twentieth century and chronicles the continued inability of established architectural norms and practices to deal with demands for shelter.

This volume does not investigate the relationship of Turkish building to examples elsewhere, nor does it shed new light on the details of the internecine arguments of various European architectural movements. The material for this collection is centered on buildings, laws and codes, criticisms and commentaries produced in Turkey from the turn of the century to 1980. It focuses on the institutions and the mechanisms for the production of architecture that have allowed the replication of the images of contemporaneity in Turkey. These images were, for the most part, those of the Western capitals, such as Berlin, Vienna and Paris of the early twentieth century and of the 1920s and 1930s and those of the United States and of reconstructed British towns of the 1950s and 1960s. But although the images of the West may have been catalysts for architectural change, the capabilities of architectural practice and the potentials of the building industry were tied to the immediate contexts of Ankara or Istanbul. Within these contexts, architectural tools, skills and attitudes were assembled from a variety of sources and were reordered to serve specifically national goals. In analyzing this body of material, it may not be sufficient to consider any building as a regional variety of the metropolitan tradition alone. Instead, the individual achievement of each building, in its internal order, and of its craftsmanship must be understood within its own setting through a critical language and criteria developed for its context.

This book concentrates on the architecture and the architectural profession of the Turkey which Atatürk created. The phenomenon of the Republic and the role of Mustafa Kemal Atatürk are common knowledge; what is perhaps less well known are the developments during the reformist decades which preceded World War I. It is during these decades that the seeds of modern Turkey were sown. This introduction will briefly review the events of these decades, with particular emphasis on the reforms within the Ottoman administration which resulted in the emergence of new classes or new elites, out of which the first professionals, among them architects, came forward.

It is generally acknowledged that modernization in Turkey began with a series of reforms collectively known as the Tanzimat (Reorganization). The era of Tanzimat was ushered in with the Imperial Edict of the Rose

Chamber (Gülhane Hatt-i Hümayunu: 1839), which proclaimed the principle of equality under law and guaranteed the security of life and property for all subjects of the Empire. Immediately thereafter, significant reform measures began to be implemented in the judicial, educational and financial spheres, and the administrative structure of the state was transformed. The Tanzimat reforms were formulated by elites with a Western orientation and constituted the first far-reaching and coherent program of adopting European institutions as models.

Educational reforms, pursued continually throughout the rest of the century, at first served to swell the ranks of the Westernized intelligentsia who contributed to the momentum of the reform movements by taking positions in the bureaucracy and later led to the creation of elite professional classes. Judicial reforms which initially aimed at establishing due process and legislating a commercial code were more difficult to achieve since they entailed a move, however gradual, away from the *shari'a*, Islamic law, on which the Ottoman system was based, toward secular, impersonal law, in which the testimony of a Muslim would not be given precedence over that of a non-Muslim. Fiscal reforms were aimed at eliminating unjust practices in taxation as well as assuring efficient means of collection revenue. In many ways, the Tanzimat reforms, formulated by the ruling elite with a view to modernizing institutions and arresting the decline of the Empire, can also be seen as a culmination of Ottoman reformism begun in the mid-seventeenth century with a more limited version of strengthening the military institutions.

While this reformism had been generated by internal forces, Western powers, notably England and France, also took an active interest in the implementation of the reform program. In the wake of the Crimean War, the powers demanded further reforms as a precondition to admit the Ottoman Empire into the Council of Europe. The Imperial Edict of 1856 reaffirmed the principles of the earlier edict but articualted more clearly and specifically certain provisions, including the equality of all Ottoman subjects. At the same time, several European countries also strengthened their role as protectors of Christian subjects in the Empire. Meanwhile, Ottoman economic dependency on Europe increased. Inflation following the Crimean War and increased expenditure for defense as well as for the expanded government required massive external borrowing. In 1863, the right to issue banknotes was conceded to the Franco-British Ottoman Bank. Twelve years later, the Sublime Porte found itself incapable of servicing its own debt and announced a partial suspension of interest payments. As a result of what amounted to the bankruptcy of the Ottoman state, the Ottoman Public Debts Administration (Düyun-i Umumiye) was established in 1881. It was this organization, administered by representatives of Britain, acting also on behalf of Dutch bond holders, and of the Governments of France, Germany, Italy, Austria and Turkey, that gained control of excise taxes and monopolies and to which other revenues were assigned later. The Düyun-i Umumiye meant European financial control and signalled the end of the Empire's economic independence.

The Tanzimat had led to a consolidation of power among the upper echelons of the bureaucracy. Secure in their position and immensely well paid, the Tanzimat elite became a self-perpetuating group. Some of its members behaved ostentatiously and displayed a pattern of conspicuous consumption and Westernized manners resembling the ways of a Western haute bourgeoisie. Reaction against these elites came from the younger intelligentsia who viewed them as an obstacle to their own promotion to the highest offices and as a group subverting the ideals of the Tanzimat. The politically motivated ones among them established the secret Young Ottoman Society in 1865 which called for greater political participation and representative government. In 1876 the first constitution was proclaimed and a parliamentary regime was established.

However, the palace also reacted to the distribution of power in the hands of the bureaucracy. Using the pretext of the Russo-Turkish War of 1877, Abdülhamit II abolished the parliament within a few months of its inception and began to implement autocratic practices in order to reassert the prerogatives of the sultanate. In the increasingly oppressive atmosphere of the next three decades, intellectuals and professionals had to choose between avoiding political activity or joining the underground opposition. Members of the reformist intelligentsia, seeking to re-establish a constitutional regime, were joined by young professionals and particularly by students in military and military-medical schools, who organized the secret cells of the Committee of Union and Progess (CUP) and collaborated with the vociferous critics of Ottoman despotism in exile. When the Young Turk revolution occured in 1908, deposing Abdülhamit II and reopening the parliament, however, it was the activist officers rather than the intellectuals who took power. The Young Turk movement had inherited the fundamental tenets of political, economic and scientific progress and the new cadres motivated by a desire to save the Ottoman Empire. Their cosmopolitan pan-Ottomanism proved futile when confronted with the increasing nationalism among the constituent elements of the Empire. Their commitment to Ottomanism was never clearly or publicly articulated, and, in fact, their government was forced, during the course of the Balkan Wars (1911-1913), to turn to Turkish nationalism as the only viable policy and ideology. The third alternative, pan-Islamism, which had been articulated in circles close to the palace during the Hamidian period in the wake of Arab nationalism, also disappeared.

The intellectual formulation of Turkish nationalism as a cohesive force was developed during the first two decades of this century. External pressures, internal disintegration, and continuous warfare hacking away the territories of a once powerful empire created a milieu conducive to a search for a new unifying ideology. Yet the implicit secularism of nationalist movements was at odds with the received notion of an Islamic community. Thus was developed what Tekeli calls the "dualist" formula of Ziya Gökalp who defined the material and scientific aspects of society as civilization and the value systems as culture. There would be in effect a dichotomy between a Turkish culture, identity and solidarity and an internationalist orientation to achieve social and scientific progress. Gökalp's formula ultimately called for an amalgam of Western civilization, Turkish polity and society, and Islam as the individual's personal belief.

World War I was effectively the end of the Ottoman Empire. Its territories were partitioned and mostly occupied. Mustafa Kemal gathered an army of volunteers in Anatolia to fight its War of Independence (1920-22) against the occupation of Anatolia by the Greeks and in 1920 convened the National Assembly in Ankara. This was the first parliament of the Turkish nation-state, while the Ottoman cabinet in Istanbul was reduced to being a shadow government in an occupied city. Having successfully ejected the occupying forces from the Aegean region and secured the integrity of the Turkish state, Mustafa Kemal embarked on his program to create a modern state. On 29 October 1923, the Republic of Turkey was proclaimed and the next year it was recognized internationally at the Lausanne Conference.

Atatürk called for faster progress and a greater degree of social cohesiveness than the Ottoman reformers had done. In addition, his modern state would break away from what was perceived as the stagnant period of Ottoman decline. Then not only were the CUP cadres replaced by Western oriented nationalists who disavowed pan-Turkism and its ambitions, but also the dualist cultural theory was replaced by a monist theory of nationalism based on citizenship. The secularizing reforms of the 1920s did not merely aim to "modernize" particular institutions one by one, but collectively they constituted a coherent program that would modernize the entire society by establishing contractual relationships under impersonal law.

Atatürk, as president of the Republic for 15 years until his death, pursued his program of reform and development. Between 1930 and 1946, Ismet Inönü, who had been a commander during the War of Independence, successfully kept Turkey out of the war, but the war years were a period of inflation, hardships and tight government control. Once the war was over, Atatürk's program of modernization was resumed. Transition to a multi-party system came in 1946 with the establishment of the Democrat Party which took power in 1950.

The last three decades witnessed the rapid growth and transition of Turkey with all the benefits and strains that are felt in the social, political and economic system during a process of rapid development.

The processes which, over several generations, sought to restructure Ottoman society and the Ottoman state had several important implications for architecture and the built environment. Their complete analysis could be the subject of a separate study. A brief indication of several of these implications seems in order here, particularly since they were important in the creation of the functions and the typology of the new setting of the Republic. For example, the reorganization of the Ottoman Empire brought with it a reorganization of its armed forces. As a result, the traditional quartering of soldiers in the precincts of the palace was replaced by a new architecture of military barracks on European models. The Palace circles turned to Western modes as well. Although the Palace had been fleetingly acquainted with the images and settings of Western royal power, it is in the Dolmabahçe (1853) that we find the introduction of the articulated Western palace with its long rectangular halls, ornate facades, ornamental window articulation and, significantly, a ballroom.

These can be cited as examples of new functions and new tastes, but the development which had a wider and more complex impact and which transformed Istanbul from a late medieval city into a far-flung commuter metropolis was the introduction of the ferryboat during the 1850s. The fact that the Şirket-i Hayriye, the Turkish-owned ferryboat company, offered housing credit in locations along the shores of the Bosporus to generate passenger traffic brought about a spurt of residential building activity. The villas built in the so-called Erenköy style were much like suburban villas elsewhere and were built for the Istanbul civil servant classes which were at this time becoming more and more Westernized.

Withal, however, the universe of building which was concentrated in Istanbul and not throughout the Empire was a limited one. There was no longer an extensive program of monumental or institutional buildings. For the Ottoman Empire there was no major rationale to transform Istanbul in the way capital cities like London, Paris, Berlin, Vienna, Rome and St. Petersburg had been. Nor were there new initiatives within the commercial or industrial sector at large. Monumental building programs had traditionally been linked to the Palace and grandee classes. The programs included the great mosques and socio-religious institutions with their revenue generating buildings. With the reform of the system of pious foundations (evkaf) through the creation of a centralized adminstrative office, the private foundation no longer appeared as a secure or worthy investment for the future of one's family. Therefore, the patron who earlier put capital into the building of public institutions now invested in land. Moreover, the inflation of land prices as well as the continued impoverishment of those classes or circles which could have built public institutions resulted in a very slowly developing construction and architectural activity.

Since the treasury had no money to build and since massive building campaigns of public works could no longer be financed by the state or by individuals, new patrons and foreign models took over. The Ottoman state could no longer issue its own currency and all of its resources were controlled through the Administration of Public Debt. The latter, controlled by Western European concerns, built its banks on the basis of a European building vocabulary of financial headquarters. Foreign investment, such as the German one in the Berlin-Baghdad railway, led to the new function of railway terminals almost as rapidly as they were developing in Europe. While the Sirkeci Railroad Terminal in Istanbul can be taken as an implantation of imperialism, it was in fact the latest product of a new function and of a technology that was in no way *retardataire* or different from railroad technology anywhere else. What was important was the difference between its impact on the building industry of Istanbul and its suburbs and the equivalent results of the Gare St. Lazare and its Parisian context. The tragedy of the Ottoman Empire at the time was that these new buildings could not in themselves be as instructive to the local building community in Istanbul as similar buildings were elsewhere.

The reason lies in the third implication of the nineteenth-century reforms, the ways in which they affected the building trade. At the level of technical cadres and craftsmen, it can be assumed that the carpenters, masons, and other construction workers issued from the traditional training system continued to practice their trade and to adapt themselves to new fashions and new needs. They were responsible for the quality of a few significant buildings such as the new military barracks and the Dolmabahçe Palace. Many of these technicians were members of minorities within the Ottoman Empire and they were also responsible for much of the new residential building activities. How the building industry and building crafts succeeded in weathering the social and ethnic upheavals during and after World War I to make a new Turkish industry is still an issue that demands investigation.

More is known about architects. The Balyan family was active as court architects until the second half of the nineteenth century. Though it issued from the traditional palace architectural school, its members did obtain European architectural training in the later years of its tenure. Then came foreigners, such as Vallaury and Jachmund. Eventually, the first Turkish architects, Kemalettin and Vedat [Bey], went to Germany or France to acquire a fully modern training. Their collective activities culminated in the creation of schools of architecture in Istanbul immediately before World War I, and of what has subsequently been called the First National Architectural Movement. The rise of these new architects cannot be understood without the milieu from which they came, which was that of the new professional elites created as an aftermath of the Tanzimat. They illustrate in a way the success of the reforms which allowed for the formation of a new intelligentsia and of a native technocracy. Just as political and military leaders such as Enver Paşa and Talat Paşa rose through the ranks of the new army, so the small group of new architects also evolved through the ambitions and ideological concerns of the Committee of Union and Progress. It is to them that the new Republican government turned initially for the planning and building of the new Turkish capital, Ankara, in remote Anatolia.

By what criteria should one judge the oeuvre of these scions of the Ottoman Empire in its last decade? When placed in the context of the careers of their classmates in the Beaux Arts or the Charlottenburg Technische Hochschule, they do not seem to have brought anything new to searches for form, from expressionist to rationalist, to building technology, brick or glass based, or even to the articulation of the architect within the development of a society. Yet to write of these individuals as merely provincial practitioners would be not to recognize their role in the cultural and social history of an emerging nation. They were the builders of new types of buildings in Turkey, hotels, multi-story apartments, railroad stations, bank and government buildings. They formed the Turkish architectural profession. They were the nuclei of the new architectural schools. They attempted to develop a regional style (The First National Movement). In short, they planted the seeds of the new architecture in the soil of the new nation state and could rightly be considered the bridges between the old world and the new.

Renata Holod and Ahmet Evin.

CHAPTER I

THE SOCIAL CONTEXT OF THE DEVELOPMENT OF ARCHITECTURE IN TURKEY

Ilhan Tekeli

This essay intends to trace the development of the contemporary architectural profession in Turkey within its social context. Three factors affect this development. First, society creates demands for particular architectural skills and functions at different stages of economic and technological evolution. Second, architects act within movements shaped by the impact of local and international architectural ideas, and in so doing they articulate an architectural ideology. Third, as the profession develops and undergoes differentiation, the means of transmitting or replacing architectural ideologies are altered. These three processes will be taken as the perimeters of our methodological framework.

In order to gain a better understanding of the development of architectural practice on these three levels, it is helpful to consider two factors in the transformation of the society. Turkey is in a process of a continuous and multi-faceted transformation under the influence of both external factors and internal dynamics. This transformation includes changes in the national economy, the emergence of new economic functions, the formation of new social institutions necessitated by these developments, changes in the class structure, and the formation of a new life-style. Thus the functions which society expects from architects are being constantly redefined, and the organization of the profession undergoes developmental changes. The transformation goes beyond the level of economic and social organization and leads to new ideological orientations. Such ideological redefinitions on the national level require architects to continually espouse new architectural movements and to reject prevailing ones.

Transformation as a determinant of change in architectural practice should be understood as a phenomenon within all peripheral countries, and not of Turkey alone. A peripheral country, when integrated into the capitalist system becomes, on the one hand, a component of international values; and on the other, confronts the problem of creating a national identity required by the ideology of nationalism which is, to a large extent, also imported from the West. If we analyze this process of incorporation of peripheral countries into the world economic system, the following questions can be answered. How does architectural practice deal with this conflict and what kind of solutions does it seek? How and under which circumstances are Western architectural trends or ideologies reinterpreted for the particular conditions within peripheral countries? Under which conditions can architects, as middle-class professionals, differ from the ideological orientations of political power groups? Under which conditions do political movements encompass architectural ideas as well?

With these questions in mind, we will explore the evolution of architectural practice in Turkey in terms of the following five periods. The first period, 1923-1927, corresponds to the continuing influence of the First National Architectural Movement which prevailed during the Second Ottoman Constitutional Period. The second is the Ankara-Vienna cubism of functional architecture between 1929-1939. The Second National Architectural Movement comprises the third period between 1940-1950. The fourth, between the years 1950-1960, is marked by International Style solutions. The fifth period after 1960 is characterized by social consciousness in architecture.

THE FIRST NATIONAL ARCHITECTURAL MOVEMENT

With the founding of the Republic following the War of Independence (1920-1922), Turkey confronted substantial structural problems, both practically and ideologically. Istanbul, the capital city for centuries, was set aside; instead Ankara was declared the new capital in spite of external pressures from the Great Powers and domestic objections from some of the country's intellectuals. This revolutionary decision rested on very significant ideological bases. A move to the interior of the country signalled a clear break away from a network of old economic dependencies. Istanbul had been a part of a network of harbor cities developed throughout the nineteenth century to serve the economic interests of the Great Powers.[1] The pattern of harbor cities, which were totally dependent on and linked to the mercantile interests of England, France and Germany, was abhorrent to the new Republicans. A move into the interior of the country was an unequivocal break with this state of dependence. Moreover, the move meant the rejection of the cosmopolitan cultural values of Istanbul. The Republic sought to release itself from the Ottoman image and to create a national bourgeoisie inculcated with Republican ideals.[2]

The development of Ankara as a modern city, which was identified with success of the Republican regime, presented the architectural profession with a major challenge. The Republican leaders turned to the protagonists of what has been designated as the First National Architectural Movement for solutions.[3] While the choice seemed natural enough, the influence of the First National Architectural Movement did not last past the initial years of capital building for a variety of reasons, not least of which was its close association with cosmopolitan, Ottoman Istanbul.

The public face of Istanbul had been shaped by influences from abroad. The Balyan family, the Armenian palace architects, designed public buildings during the reign of Abdülmecit (1839-1861), according to models they had acquired during their professional training in Europe. With the reign of Abdülhamit II (1876-1908), foreign architects began to be commissioned for major works.[4] Vallaury, who built the Public Debts Administration Building (Düyun-i Umumiye Idaresi) (Figs. 10-12), and Jachmund, who built the Sirkeci Railroad Terminal (Figs. 1, 7), shaped the new Ottoman architecture. These two architects employed elements borrowed from Ottoman-Islamic architecture on the facades of their buildings, with the aim of finding harmony with the existing environment. Various explanations can be provided for this eclecticism.

These architects had been designing in Europe in the Neoclassical tradition, using Greek and Roman forms on their facades. This eclecticism was reinterpreted by the incorporation of Ottoman-Islamic elements, in a period of commitment to the ideology of Islamism during the reign of Abdülhamit II. Yet, there was no specific demand by the Sultan or by the ideology of Islamism for such a reinterpretation of European Neoclassicism to fit particular local conditions. It is not even certain whether there had ever been any particular interest in encouraging such a style. Rather the demand might have come from the owners of these buildings, foreign companies which may have hoped somehow to gain greater acceptance.

Fig. 1 Jachmund, Sirkeci Railroad Terminal, Istanbul, 1890. Detail of main entry.

The new buildings were curious because they did not resemble the building types that existed in Ottoman society prior to the nineteenth century. One was the headquarters of foreign capital control in Turkey; the other a railroad terminal. They were the architectural representations of new functions which were the result of industrialization and of integration into the world economy. No sign of such eclecticism is evident in residential architecture. The upper strata, chiefly Ottoman bureaucracy, exhibited a preference for the so-called "Erenköy Style," which Sedat Eldem finds akin to the Victorian styles. At the same time, segments of the Greek and Armenian population, consisting chiefly of entrepreneurs and small merchants, built Greco-Roman style houses most commonly found on the Izmir waterfront.[5]

The new eclecticism had a substantial impact on the developing architectural profession. A training program, independent of engineering, was started in the Academy of Fine Arts (Sanayi-i Nefise Mektebi) which had been established in 1882. Meanwhile the School of Civil Engineering (Hendese-i Mülkiye), which had been established in 1884, provided an architectural education as yet undifferentiated from engineering.[6] Vallaury was teaching in the former, and Jachmund in the latter. Kemalettin Bey, the acknowledged founder of the First National Architectural Movement, had been a student of Jachmund. After graduating in 1891, he was appointed as an assistant to his teacher. In 1896, Kemalettin Bey was sent to the Charlottenburg Technische Hochschule in Berlin where he studied architecture for two years. He then worked for several architects before returning to Turkey in 1900.[7] The second person who played a pioneering role in the development of the First National Architectural Movement, Vedat [Tek], had received his architectural education in the prominent Ecole Nationale des Beaux Arts before returning to Turkey in 1897.[8] Back in Turkey, Kemalettin Bey and Vedat [Tek] began teaching at the School of Civil Engineering and the Academy of Fine Arts, respectively. In their lectures, they formulated the principles of an architecture based on the use of Ottoman-Islamic elements and trained a small cadre of young architects. Prior to 1908, however, their practice was limited; the only significant example was the Central Post Office by Vedat [Tek] (Figs. 15-17).

In 1908, under the initiative of the Committee of Union and Progress, the second Ottoman Constitutional Assembly was established. Inspired by the Constitutional regime, the Society of Ottoman Architects and Engineers was founded on August 15. Of its twenty-one members eleven were architects, three of whom were Turks.[9] However, this society soon became instrumental in providing Turkish architects with access to political circles and in securing commissions for them, especially after 1912 when nationalism emerged as the predominant ideology in the Committee of Union and Progress.

To some extent owing to his personal connections, Vedat [Tek] was appointed Chairman of the Supervising Committee for Public Works (Heyet-i Fenniye Reisi) during the time of Cemal Topuzlu Paşa, the mayor of Istanbul, and later Chief Architect (Baş Mimar) during the reign of Mehmet Reşat. Kemalettin Bey was put in charge of the Supervising Committee of the Ministry of Pious Foundations (Evkaf Nezareti Heyet-i

Fenniyesi). The Ministry had undergone significant reforms and had begun undertaking the most extensive building activity of the period. Both architects proved effective in propagating their architectural ideas. They disseminated their ideas through educational institutions, introduced them to professional circles through their Society, and implemented them in a dual practice through their new supervisory positions.

These architectural ideas, although now equipped with the means to reproduce themselves, did not yet have a specific name; their designation as "National Movement" did not come until the Balkan War of 1912. The defeat in this war, the loss of the Balkans, and the Albanian uprising resulted in the bankrupcy of pan-Ottomanism and pan-Islamism. It was then that the Committee of Union and Progress espoused Turkish nationalism.[10] The urban institutional architecture which had developed with an Ottoman-Islamic face was now also called nationalist.

The chief ideologue of Turkish nationalism was Ziya Gökalp. He based his ideology upon a bi-partite cultural theory: "civilization" (*medeniyet*), which consisted largely of scientific and technological knowledge, was international in character and could easily be adopted from the West; "culture" (*hars*), which included particular national traits and could not be borrowed from elsewhere, could only be derived from a nation's history and be perpetuated by its people. Accordingly, Ottoman modernization would be based on adopting European civilization while retaining Turkish identity and the Islamic religion.[11]

Just as the cultural tenets of Turkish nationalism had international and indigenous components, its economic program, articulated later during World War I, was shaped on the one hand by German Romantic economic thought from Müller to Schmoller and on the other hand by the growing dictatorial ambitions of the Committee of Union and Progress. As a result state and society were elevated, and the individual was demoted.

Thus, when the political developments of the Ottoman Empire produced a nationalist movement, they at the same time coopted an already existing architecture and dubbed it the First National Architectural Movement. This movement can be analyzed according to Ziya Gökalp's bi-partite cultural theory. Buildings such as the Post Office (Figs. 15-17), Pious Foundations' Office Buildings (Vakıf Hanı) (Figs. 23-25, 37-38), the Imperial Offices of Land Registry (Defter-i Hakani) (Fig. 18), belonged to institutions introduced into the Ottoman Empire through its incorporation into the capitalist world economy. In the construction of these buildings, modern structural systems such as steel or reinforced concrete were employed. While the organization of functions and masses was borrowed from the West, elements such as arches, columns, mouldings, cantilevers, and overhangs, derived from the examples of classical Ottoman architecture, were used in the treatment of the exterior. The synthesis sought in architecture corresponded to Ziya Gökalp's duality of "civilization" and "culture."

Although the Movement gained legitimacy and acceptance among Turkish architects, its application was essentially limited to public buildings. For a brief period some leaders of the Committee of Union and Progress tried to force this national style on housing, but no such measures were ever implemented.

When Ankara was established as the capital, the First National Architectural Movement was the dominant architectural style. In addition to Kemalettin Bey and Vedat [Tek], the buildings of the new Republic were designed by Arif Hikmet, Halim, Ahmet Kemal, Tahsin Sermet, Ali Talât, Fatih Ülkü, Mehmet Nihat, and Giulio Mongeri, a proponent of national architecture who taught in the Academy of Fine Arts.[12] Until 1927, not only the large-scale public buildings but also the houses of Ankara were

Fig. 2 Vedat [Tek] and Kemalettin Bey, Ankara Palas Hotel, 1924-1927.

built according to the style. Buildings constructed within this five-year period in no way conveyed the image of a Western city. Ahmet Haşim, prominent poet and critic, criticizes these developments in *Gurabahane-i Lâklâkan* (1928):

> Ever since young poets have started to compose in the modern meter and ever since some have started to conduct the music of Turkish *saz* with a baton, a *medrese* architecture, to which we are unable to assign a name, has spread among our architects. Hotel, bank, school, port-house are each a caricature of a mosque, with a "minaret" missing on the outside, and a "minbar" on the inside. Our architects call this style of building "Turkish architecture."[13]

The reproduction of the Ottoman religious buildings was inconsistent with the goals of the Republican leaders who wanted to rid themselves of both Ottoman and Islamic images. Furthermore, the National Architectural Movement was largely identified with the Committee of Union and Progress. The leaders of the Republic engineered a removal of the Committee members from the political arena because that last generation of Ottoman modernizers sought to achieve a synthesis of East and West, whereas the Republicans were adamant Westernists. Naturally they would turn against an architectural style in Ottoman vestments. Moreover, the death of Kemalettin Bey in 1927, and the departure of Vedat [Tek] from Ankara, after a dispute concerning the construction of the Ankara Palas Hotel, undermined the strength of the Movement (Figs. 2, 32-36). Ultimately the failure of the National Architectural Movement stems from its inability to develop a city planning proposal. The Movement dealt mainly with formal and stylistic issues, and had not developed city planning capabilities.

Given the unplanned growth of Ankara, how was the desired modern city image to be achieved? Beginnings of city planning ideas were already in circulation. In the 1920s the mayor of Istanbul, Dr. Emin, formed a circle of people interested in city planning and began publishing a journal of city administration (*Istanbul Şehremaneti Mecmuası*) as well as the first translations of books on city planning. Notwithstanding the fact that within the Istanbul municipal circles there existed Sittean tendencies which could easily have been articulated into national architectural ideas, such a development did not occur.[14]

The combination of factors thus far listed oriented the Republic towards a search for the universal rather than the national. Foreign architects were invited to work on individual buildings as well as on city planning.

CUBISM OR THE PERIOD OF FUNCTIONAL ARCHITECTURE (1927-1939)

The Bauhaus Movement which developed in the wake of World War I advocated simplicity, economy, functionalism, and materialism in architecture as opposed to eclectic or Neoclassical attitudes. It viewed the art of building as the "melting-pot" of all the other arts and called for a collaboration among all of them. In this context, city planning was conceived as having a close relationship to architecture. Exponents of the

Modern Movement, such as Pieter Oud, Mies Van der Rohe, Walter Gropius, Le Corbusier, Bruno Taut, Eric Mendelsohn, Theo Van Doesburg, and Ernst May, began to diffuse it as an international movement in the congresses of CIAM. The design principles of this universalistic creed were derived from the premises of technology, materials and geometry.[15]

The development of an architectural movement in Europe deemphasizing the national dimension on the one hand and the emergence of a "monist" cultural theory in Turkey on the other facilitated the acceptance of the Modern Movement in Turkey. Turkish nationalism was reinterpreted in the 1930s to allow for an internationalist orientation. Two theories advanced in this period, the Sun Language Theory and the History Thesis, sought to establish common origins with Western culture and civilization. Furthermore, the design philosophy of the Modern Movement based upon technology, function, materials, and geometry was in line with the positivism of the Republicans.

The four European architects who came to Ankara prior to 1930, Theodor Post, Ernst Egli, Clemens Holzmeister, and Hermann Jansen, were, however, not leading figures of the Bauhaus Movement. The most active practicioner, Holzmeister, was more of a representative of the Vienna School. Sedat Eldem views the work of these architects in Ankara as a type of an Ankara-Vienna cubist architecture whose characteristics he describes:

> Plans and elevations revealed themselves in their ornament-free lines and surfaces. Pitched roofs, tiles and eaves were eliminated. To be modern, a building could not have a hat. Because this architecture was realized in Ankara, it was built in the locally available material rather than continuing the use of plastered stone. Thus the dark colored Ankara stone became prevalent. A type of plaster, the so-called terra-nova, peculiar to German countries, was also imitated. It was applied in the required mass and thickness according to German taste; surfaces were textured rather than smooth. The plaster was greyish and the stone was purplish. The proportions and details of the windows were completely changed; traditional French and Mediterranean forms were replaced by German style proportions and details. Aesthetics were radically transformed.[16]

Between 1927-1930, the Ministry of Health (Fig. 54) was designed by Theodor Post; the Court of Financial Appeals (Fig. 61) and the Ismet Paşa Institute for Girls (Fig. 62) by Ernst Egli; the Ministry of National Defense (Fig. 55), the Institute of Agriculture, the Officers' Club (Fig. 58), and the General Staff Building (Fig. 56) by Holzmeister.[17]

These three architects, as well as Hermann Jansen, the winner of the restricted competition for the city master plan, shaped the face of Ankara. The fact that they could do so bespoke the real weakness of the protagonists of the First National Movement. In addition, the movement lost out to these newcomers in the educational field. In 1926, the Academy of Fine Arts was reorganized as Güzel Sanatlar Mektebi. And by 1930, the studios of Vedat [Tek] and Mongeri, responsible for nurturing the movement, were closed. Instead, Ernst Egli was given authority over architectural curricula.[18]

The Modern Movement in architecture was influential not only in public buildings, but also in the design of houses. Although European furniture had been introduced into the residences of the upper classes in the Ottoman Empire, it was not yet widespread among the lower strata. The Republic brought the change down to the middle classes. The divan (*sedir, kerevet*) and the tray table (*tabla, sini*) within residences gave way to Western style furniture. This was a far more radical change than simply replacing one type of furniture with another. It demanded a simultaneous transition from the Ottoman house containing unspecialized spaces to a house consisting of different, specialized rooms. Western furniture brought with it the notion of specialized space in house design. Functionalist architecture provided the means for this change in the house form.

The diffusion of the Modern Movement was made possible by the key supervisory role of foreign architects in the considerable building programs of the Republic. In general, Turkish architects, however, did not advocate an architectural movement different from that which the foreign architects had introduced. Their efforts were focused in two directions: first, to organize themselves and expand their professional market through legislation, and secondly, to prove that Turkish architects could achieve as much in modern architecture as the foreigners.[19]

In 1927, the Association of Turkish Architects (Türk Yüksek Mimarlar Derneği) was established in Ankara and the Union of Fine Arts (Güzel Sanatlar Birliği) in Istanbul. With the Engineering and Architectural Services Act (Public Law 1035), practice in these fields was reserved to holders of diplomas beginning in June 1928. In 1931 the first architectural journal in Turkey, *Mimar*, was founded. It published works in the Modern Style by Turkish architects. Meanwhile, architects educated in Europe began promoting their designs by exhibiting them in Ankara. Nevertheless, their efforts met with very limited success until 1929.

By 1930, as the impact of the Depression was felt in Turkey, one of the immediate reponses was the establishment of the National Economy and Savings Society. With the support of the state, this association began launching extensive campaigns to provide incentives for the consumption of domestic commodities and to condemn the consumption of foreign products. It organized "domestic commodities" weeks. The ideological milieu created by such campaigns was favorable for Turkish architects to defend their professional market. As a part of these campaigns, the National Economy and Savings Society decided to commission an Exhibition Building where domestic commodities would be displayed. For the design of the building, an international competition was organized. It was not a mere coincidence that a Turkish architect, Şevki [Balmumcu], won the first prize (Fig. 80).[20] Later Nejat Bey won the competition for the Bursa Atatürk Monument and Nazmi Yaver Bey for the interior design for the Balkan Entente Conference.[21] These successes emboldened Turkish architects to demand the organization of competitions for scheduled buildings (Fig. 3).

Fig. 3 Akalın, Railroad Terminal, Ankara, 1937.

The political, economic and ideological reorientation in the wake of the Depression did not induce changes in the accepted architectural ideas, but resulted instead in an increased share of the market for Turkish architects. On the whole, their attitude toward their foreign colleagues was not negative. Even Şevki [Balmumcu] acknowledged the need for the latter.[22] However, these architects were to be limited to the field of education, leaving the realm of practice to Turkish architects. Since the latter conceived the issue as a problem of economic redistribution rather than of architectural ideology, they were ready to abandon architectural education to foreigners. Yet neither the numbers nor the political power of Turkish architects were sufficient to dominate the building arena. After 1933, architects and city planners fleeing Hitler's regime would assume significant roles both in educational institutions and in practice. Among them, there were such prominent names as Bruno Taut, Martin Wagner and Gustav Oelsner.[23]

This implantation of a contemporary life-style, much desired by the leaders of the Republic, had to be conceived both on the level of new individual buildings and on the larger scale of city planning. The Republican cadres had not inherited a city planning tradition. City planning in the Ottoman Empire had been based essentially on the replanning of districts after the destruction of wooden buildings by frequent fires and the widening of the streets within the traditional texture to accommodate new vehicles. These measures did not constitute a sufficient experience to direct the establishment of a capital city. Between 1928 and 1933, the preferences of the Republic on this issue were further articulated.

After initial pragmatic implementations and an unsuccessful planning effort, Republican leaders chose to commission the planning of Ankara through a restricted competition.[24] Two of the three invited competitors were German. Hermann Jansen, the winner of the Berlin Plan competition, was an architect with Sittean experience. Brix was teaching in the Charlottenburg Technische Hochschule. The third competitor, Jaussely, was educated in the Ecole des Beaux Arts. He had won the competition for the Barcelona plan and had implemented it. And he had also won first prize in the 1919 Paris Planning Competition. Having turned to the West, the Republic had not found a single solution there. The opinions fluctuated between Jaussely's impressive, grand capital city design in the French tradition and Jansen's Sittean, more modest, socially and historically conscious plan. The jury, dominated by Republican leaders and their followers, chose Jansen's plan. Was this a manifestation of the preference for Central European approaches in Republican city planning?

It is not possible to give a sure answer. Later, the Republican leaders would assign the planning of Trabzon and Erzurum to Lambert, and of Istanbul in 1936 to Prost, both eminent French planners. In this context, an analysis of the 1933 Buildings and Roads Act might provide a clue. This act listed detailed requirements for the form of city plans, and can therefore be considered as an indicator of the Republic's image of the city. The grid-iron pattern required by this act bears no relation to the French planning tradition, nor to the Sittean approach. These inconsistencies suggest that the Republic did not have a single set of ideologically derived criteria.

While there was no particular preference among schools of city planning, the choices pertaining to the organization of planning were nevertheless consistent with the nature of the regime. With the 1933 Municipal Public Works Act, it obliged municipalities to develop and implement master plans. With the 1933 Buildings and Roads Act, it defined city plans in minute detail, almost after a model. The making and supervision of these plans was centralized through the Municipalities Planning Council (Belediye Imar Heyeti) and City Planning Supervisory Council, Ministry of Public Works (Bayındırlık Bakanlığı Şehircilik Fen Heyeti). The financing of these programs was also centralized through the establishment of the Municipalities' Bank. Hence a city planning network was created in which plans were made and supervised centrally but implemented by the municipalities. The model was consistent with a single party fully devoted to the principle of rapid modernization. But it dissociated city planning from the municipality and therefore from practice.[25]

Thus, the plans made in this period were shaped more by the city schemes demanded by the regime than by the actual problems of cities and considerations of implementation. Consequently, the tendency to import plans from the West was further strengthened.

SECOND NATIONAL ARCHITECTURAL MOVEMENT (1940-1950)

Even as the Modern Movement continued to dominate the building and planning programs of the new Republic throughout the period 1927-1939, forces were gathering to oppose it. The construction problems of the cubist buildings, particularly their flat, perpetually leaking roofs, did much to taint their image. The planned city was now perceived as an alien environment. As Sedat Eldem once expressed it, dark eaveless buildings inserted into the heart of every settlement and streets drawn with a T-square and lined with willows were changing the face of the Anatolian towns.

Because of the Depression, the government began searching for a new economic order. In 1932, Ankara suddenly strengthened its ties with the Soviet Union and with Italy, and began preparing the First Industrial Five-Year Plan on the Soviet Model. Books informing the Turkish people about the achievements of the Soviet and the Italian regimes began to appear.[26] They reflected a new nationalism and were based on the primacy of the state. Reaction against the internationalist Modern Movement mounted. The 1934 Italian Fascist Architecture Exhibition in Ankara had a considerable impact. By 1943 the popularity of fascist architecture reached a climax with the German Architectural Exhibition. Under these influences, Turkish architects turned away from universal approaches toward monumentalizing national ones. In fact, they demanded the formulation of a national architectural policy. It should be remembered that even in Roosevelt's America similar calls for a national architecture were heard.[27]

The new ideologies led to major changes in the curricula of architectural education. In 1934, Eldem began his Seminar on National Architecture in the Academy of Fine Arts.[28] The approach of this seminar differed from the search for a national architecture in the period of Kemalettin Bey and Vedat [Tek] in two important ways. First, the seminar focused on Ottoman civic rather than religious architecture. Second, it attempted to formulate a set of principles independent of particular building types or their individual elements. These became the principles on which the national architecture was to be based. The turn to civic architecture was caused by the realization that reviving the images of Ottoman religious architecture would never be allowed in secular Republican Turkey. Although this seminar would turn to the Anatolian house and seek a more populist context in the 1940s, it is difficult to observe any populism in its early stages. Interest was centered on the residences, *konaks, köşks* and *yalıs,* of the Istanbul upper classes. This choice can also be understood as the reaction of the old cosmopolitan Istanbul culture to the new culture of Ankara; or differently put, an expression of Ottoman elitism.

The search for an essence or for a set of invariable principles was shaped by two major factors. In developing a purely national architecture, there was the need on the one hand to avoid the criticism of Ottomanism, eclecticism and superficiality which had been leveled at the representatives of the First National Movement. On the other hand, there was the necessity to prove that this new national expression was as modern and as universal as the principles of the Modern Movement. Such constraints led researchers to seek fixed proportions and invariant plan types and to abstract architectural analyses from their social determinants. How such an abstraction complicates the defense of proposed projects will be discussed later. This abstraction had a justification also in terms of the Movement's desired pragmatic ends. The aim was not to design Turkish houses, but to control the design of the public buildings of the Republic. The major figure of the Movement, Sedat Eldem, advocated *dirigisme* in architecture. If the architectural principles articulated through research were abstract enough, their application to public buildings would be possible even though they had been evolved from residential architecture. This National Architectural Movement yielded its first significant product after Atatürk's death, with Sedat Eldem's prize-winning design for the Turkish pavilion in the 1939 New York Exposition.[29]

Following this first example, the Second National Architectural Movement gained momentum. In 1937, an architectural department was established in the Istanbul Engineering School, graduating its first class in 1940. This school would evolve into Istanbul Technical University in 1946, and the Department of Architecture into a separate faculty within it. Under the influence of both new European interpretations and the new ideological atmosphere in Turkey, foreign professors teaching in this school helped reinforce the same approaches. Significant contributions were made by Clemens Holzmeister, who began teaching at the Engineering School in 1940, by Paul Bonatz, who began teaching in Istanbul Technical University in 1946, and by Gustav Oelsner, who held the chair of city planning there. To the efforts of Sedat Eldem should be added the works of André Gabriel, the French archeologist and architectural historian, and the research of Bruno Taut, who began teaching in the Academy in 1937.

Assistants in both schools focused their dissertation work on the collection of Turkish vernacular architectural forms. All theses at Istanbul Technical University dwelt on some aspect of Anatolian architecture, such as houses, bath houses or marketplaces. Elements of traditional architecture were deemed necessary in government buildings as well as in Peoples' Houses, the cultural arm of the single-party regime. Competitions organized by the Ministry of Public Works helped disseminate the new ideology among architects. Buildings thought to be in keeping with the principles of the Second National Architectural Movement won these competitions. For aspiring young architects the road to success lay in conforming with the aesthetic values of the Movement. As the most influential member of these juries, Bonatz ensured the outcome of these competitions.

Despite its wide acceptance, the Movement had a rather loose framework open to very different interpretations. Four distinct approaches can be discerned. The first one is the *regionalist* approach, according to which national architecture had to conform to local materials and climatic conditions of the country, and had to exhibit a cultural continuity in order to match its environment. Earlier Turkish art had to be thoroughly analyzed to arrive at a regional synthesis. Bruno Taut can be counted among the supporters of this approach. The second approach can be characterized as being *nostalgic*, calling for the glorification of the past. However, it was not a search for grandeur or glory; it only claimed that the values of the past were still valid. Gabriel argued that Istanbul houses were actually modern and would yield better results than cubist architecture if only wood were to be replaced by concrete.[30] Similar attitudes may be found in the *konak* and *köşk* architecture of Sedat Eldem. The third approach whose inspiration derived not from the Istanbul upperclass environment, but from Anatolia can be named *populist*. Values rising out of the anonymous and continuous processes of Anatolian life were of

Fig. 4 Uçar, State Railroads Headquarters (T.C.D.D. Genel Müdürlüğü), Ankara, 1941.

utmost importance. Oelsner's efforts to recreate Anatolian life patterns in an urban environment are representative of this approach.[31] The fourth approach can be called *chauvinist*. The emphasis was on grandeur and monumentality in building. The past was also conceived in these terms.[32]

These four tendencies existed simultaneously in varying degrees. Hence, very different kinds of buildings have been accepted as representative of this movement: the State Railroad Headquarters (Figs. 4, 73), the Atatürk Mausoleum (Anıtkabir) (Fig. 82), the Faculty of Science Buildings in Istanbul and Ankara Universities (Figs. 74, 76), the Saraçoğlu Quarter (Fig. 147), the Çanakkale Unknown Soldier Monument, and the Oriental Café (Şark Kahvesi). The Oriental Café is one example of the Movement's confusion of values. Its very name was contradictory to the essence of the Republic and of the Movement, though it actually served as a high-class restaurant for the Westernized Turkish elite. In this respect it was closer in function and conception to the Viennese café than to the traditional Turkish one. It is possible to detect in this name an effort to conceal elitism behind the nostalgic and populist concepts of the nationalist movement. An ideological confusion indeed!

The confusion not only pertained to the ideological dimension, but also to the Movement's perception and use of history. Within the ideology of the Republic there was no nostalgia for the Ottoman past. Therefore it was necessary to go further back. The Seljuk period proved to be more acceptable and more fruitful. And, because the official History Thesis extended "Turkishness" all the way back to Hittite and Mesopotamian civilizations, it was now possible to go back to these periods in the search for monumentality as was the case with the Atatürk Mausoleum.

An architectural movement involving such diverse and contradictory elements resulted in confusing rather than unifying the architects. This was frankly expressed by a follower of the Movement, Abidin Mortaş, who said in 1941: "What is the modern national architecture which we demand from Turkish architects supposed to be? In this respect, we do not yet have the vaguest notion."[33] The journal *Mimar*, in an attempt to identify the

National Architectural Movement, distributed in 1944 a questionnaire on the topic. The central idea emerging from the answers was that a national architecture, not evident in the buildings constructed thus far, was yet to come.[34]

Although it had emerged as a reaction to the Modern Movement, the Second National Movement had in no way rejected modernism. It viewed itself as being modern. The nostalgic approach found modernity in historic exemplars. The regionalist approach presented regionalism as the precondition of modernism and rationalism. The chauvinist approach, in its search for the impressive, reinforced its essentially modern tendencies with monumental elements. In fact, this movement would survive only by espousing modernism.

Open criticism of the Movement began as early as 1945. For example, the Saraçoğlu Quarter of Paul Bonatz was criticized as follows: "National architecture ... does not mean borrowing elements from traditional buildings that seem beautiful to us today and attaching them onto new buildings such as Bonatz has done. Such new buildings cannot respond to our requirements. Today's Turkish architecture is an architecture trying to answer contemporary needs...." Turkish architects were annoyed not only by the formal answers of the Movement but also by the ascendancy of foreign architects within it. Adnan Kuruyazıcı asked: "How can foreigners become 'national' in three months when an architect who lived here all his life is not?"[35]

By the late 1940s there were over 300 practicing architects in Turkey. They could now form an effective lobby to exclude foreign architects from practice. For example, in 1949, the decision to give the commission for the Medical School Project of Istanbul University to foreign architects met with organized protest.[36] The architects were able to act as a pressure group protecting their own professional territory within the new democratic atmosphere. Ironically, even while such nationalist pressures began to mount, the Second National Architectural Movement was being abandoned for the International Style.

THE SEARCH FOR INTERNATIONAL SOLUTIONS THROUGH FORMS (1950-1960)

That Turkey was going to pursue a new economic policy after World War II was evident when it signed the Bretton-Woods Agreement. The introverted autarchic economic growth model adopted after 1929 was abandoned in favor of liberal economic policies. The priority given to industrial development was now directed to agriculture, and the infrastructure policy based upon railroads was being replaced by one aiming to develop highways. The new policies aimed to give the private sector a larger part in development.

The nature of the demand for buildings changed considerably during this period. First, the rapid mechanization of agriculture and the demobilization of the army freed millions who then flocked to the cities. Until the 1950s the capital, Ankara, had been growing at a rate of six percent annually but other cities at a much lesser pace. Now, however, all cities began growing at a rate of six percent. Ankara began losing its primacy. Second, the private sector was now gaining strength and was beginning to set the taste in buildings through its commissions. Yet, more public buildings were constructed during this period than in preceding periods. The search for form in Turkish architecture would still be determined by buildings erected for public institutions.

Solutions to the building demands in all fields were determined either by the domestic policies and the international relationships of the new regime or by the manner in which Westernization had come to be interpreted. Public institutions could no longer be represented in the old authoritarian manner because the newly established Democrat Party had developed a new interpretation of populism and looked upon the masses as its potential source of votes. The earlier motto, "in spite of the people, for the people," justified by the goal of modernization during the single-party regime, was now replaced by a populist approach seemingly respectful of people's choices and anti-bureaucratic sentiments. The meaning of "West" in Turkey also changed. Prior to World War II, "West" for Turkey was essentially Europe. After the War, the United States emerged as the leader of the West. Accordingly, the Democrat Party leaders aimed to make Turkey a small America. American influence was felt in the economic sphere through the effects of international market mechanisms. But Turkey's orientation toward the United States did not entail a deliberate cultural choice or philosophical preference on the part of leadership.

Both the new populist attitude dominating the political arena and the international orientation of Turkey had an impact on public building. After World War II, along with architects such as Mies Van der Rohe and Walter Gropius, the U.S.A. imported the Modern Movement of Europe and reinterpreted it for its own conditions. Meanwhile, in post-War Europe, the reconstruction of destroyed cities and the efforts to provide housing favored new proposals for cheap and industrialized construction, like that of Le Corbusier. British planners were most active in implementing plans for new cities.

This revived architectural search in the West on the one hand, and the new demands in Turkey rising out of political changes on the other, caused Turkish architects to abandon the search for a national architecture. An early sign of the new attitude was the competition for the Istanbul Palace of Justice (Adliye Sarayı). The project by Sedat Eldem and Emin Onat was the winner (Fig. 84). These two influential professors, one at the Academy of Fine Arts and the other at Istanbul Technical University, had been pioneers of the National Architectural Movement. Yet, they were the first to abandon it by entering the competition with an internationalist project.[37]

The construction of the Istanbul Hilton Hotel introduced the new American architectural design and practice along with American management. The commission for the hotel was executed by Skidmore, Owings and Merrill with Eldem as their only Turkish collaborator (Figs. 85, 86).

The International Style became dominant after 1952. Government buildings, commissioned through competitions, acquired geometrical plans with grid patterns and modular principles employed on the facades. Among the masters of modern architecture, Mies Van der Rohe and Le Corbusier were particularly influential. Although rationalism was the dominant strain in the beginning, freer forms emerged later, paralleling the developments in the West.[38] In the expression of architectural form, key concepts such as organic, modular, organism-like, brutalist, were frequently encountered. Turkish architects were no longer bound by ideological constraints and could readily adopt changing Western solutions and trends in form.[39] Is it justified to regard these architects as imitative and not creative (Fig. 5)? The International Style was espoused in Turkey by architects who had been formed by the ideology of the National Architectural Movement. But these architects now abandoned the latter. One of the reasons must have been the impossibility of continuing a national architecture in a peripheral country integrated politically and economically into the international order. It may have been easier to pursue the course of a national architecture in closed economic and political systems, but it is not very realistic to expect the development of an influential international style in a peripheral country. Contemporary means of communication and the international architectural press did not and do not normally recognize such developments. In these circumstances, probably the only realistic strategy for the architects of peripheral countries is to respond to market demands by demonstrating their ability to follow Western models, and to defend their professional market within the country against outsiders.

The Chamber of Architects, established in 1954, served to increase the control of the architects in the distribution of public commissions. The control of architectural competitions, the most important means of directing and reinforcing architectural styles, was now bound by new rules which gave greater powers to the Chamber. As a result, the state no longer solely controlled the creation of public architecture. The socio-economic status of architects was enhanced by the rise in construction activity and by the expansion of the professional market.

Fig. 5 Tekeli, Sisa and Hepgüler, Complex of Retail Shops (Manifaturacılar Çarşısı), Istanbul, 1959.

Architectural education was slow to reflect these changes. There was no sudden increase in the number of architectural schools. It was only in 1956 that the Architectural Department of the Middle East Technical University was established to offer a program of study following the prevailing trends of the period. It was modelled after American universities and, at the beginning, the University of Pennsylvania contributed to its development.

In general, however, both the organizational achievements of architects and their preferences among different architectural styles were totally marginal to the internal dynamics of Turkish society. Rapid urbanization generated its own rules and mobilized different social forces in creating a new living environment. Neither architects nor other professionals were able to play any role in this process. They only tried to retain their professional monopoly and to ensure their elitist, urban identity.

Rapid urbanization engendered two completely new building processes which limited the effectiveness of architects in shaping the environment. The first new building process was the *gecekondu*. The incoming uprooted rural masses were forming ever-widening squatter belts around the cities. The building practices modelled after Western building rules were incapable of providing these groups with shelter. These practices were based on complex bureaucratic methods and on the assumption that buildings are constructed as a whole. They were not suited to the economic resources of the newcomers nor to their lack of familiarity with the urban institutions. The incoming masses devised squatter building by relying upon their own skills, on the possibilities of the market and on patronage. This social development was viewed as a problem among the professional circles of middle-class origin; whereas the masses, also exploiting the new populist tendencies of political circles, had solved a problem that defied solution within the professional ethos.

The functions that this solution fulfilled, in terms of industrialization particularly after the 1960s, have to be kept in mind. While professional circles decried these squatter settlements, industrialists looked upon them most favorably. This new living environment reduced the cost of labor recruitment and made the provision of cheap labor easier for the industry. Hence both the new immigrants and those employing them viewed the squatter house as a solution.

The second process limiting the effectiveness of architects was commercial (*yapsatçılık*) development. As a result of urbanization and of speculation, the land values in the planned sections of the city were so high that it became impossible for middle classes to own single family houses on individual lots. In this situation, "flat-ownership" (*kat mülkiyeti*) was institutionalized, allowing the middle classes to buy individual apartments. Small entrepreneurs, known as "builders-and-sellers," initiated the formation of very densely built up districts in the planned sections of cities by building multi-storey buildings. An unusual feature of the Turkish contractor was that he did not invest any of his own capital in the process but served only as a middleman between the lot owner and the potential buyers of individual flats. In this process, the designer and the user had no contact; the encounter was between the designer and the contractor. Buildings were designed to sell. Market tastes, largely determined by the traditional sectors of the middle classes engaged in retail trade and commerce, predominated. The criteria of the contractor were imposed on the architect. In time, some architects became contractors as well but were equally constrained by market tastes.

While professionals could not restrict or in any way change unplanned urban growth, the state was forced to take some limited measures to direct it. A new Planning Expropriation Act was passed in 1956; squatter houses built before a particular date were legitimized; and the Ministry of Reconstruction and Settlement was established in 1958. Yet, the outward-oriented economic policies pursued by the Democrat Party government had left Turkey with substantial economic bottlenecks after 1955. The Menderes government had pinned its hopes on foreign aid to overcome these bottlenecks. Unable to obtain such aid, the regime became increasingly repressive against rising internal opposition, and simultaneously began to seek popular support by launching large-scale planning and construction operations in Istanbul. These operations in reality had nothing to do with the problems of squatter housing; they were totally focused on the traditional texture of the city. They consisted of widening streets, and of clearing the surroundings of some historical religious monuments and restoring them.

Architects were as much opposed to the haphazard urban growth as to the government's exploitation of city planning issues for political ends. Because they had been organized as a professional lobby, they were able to take a public stand for the first time in Turkey. What they criticized most was in fact true: this large-scale and politically motivated construction activity was far from providing solutions to any problems of urbanization or to the preservation of the historical environment or the city planning issues.

DIFFUSION OF SOCIAL CONSCIOUSNESS AFTER 1960

Since the 1960s multi-faceted developments have taken place in Turkey, determining architectural practice and thinking. Let us first describe these developments and then analyze their impact on architectural practice.

The Democrat Party regime ended when the government was taken over by the Armed Forces on May 27, 1960. After the restoration of democracy, a liberal new constitution was prepared. Leftist groups were allowed to function for the first time in the country's political life. Embracing the notion of the welfare state, the 1961 Constitution opened the doors for socialist thinking and introduced the State Planning Organization. This institution was established with the idea that scientific development planning could be achieved outside the realm of politics. Planning helped the social sciences to acquire the status of positive sciences, which could then be used in formulating policies and orienting activities. Social sciences were no longer conceived as instruments for transmitting ideology. Efforts to base architecture on the foundations of social sciences multiplied, largely through the programs in the Architecture and in the City and Regional Planning Departments of the Middle East Technical University.

By diffusing the notion of planning at all levels, the State Planning

Organization made architects increasingly aware that a decision-making hierarchy existed in society and that this hierarchy, extending from the individual building to the entire country, determined architectural design.

Recognition of the social determinants of the architectural product led to the inclusion of social sciences in architectural curricula. Yet it was also realized that scientific pursuit was not as neutral as was generally asssumed. The earlier positivist vision of science was substantially shaken by criticism from the left. Consequently, those advocating a scientific basis for architectural education encountered a major problem—the problem of selecting among different approaches. Those with positivist inclinations both tried to introduce quantitative techniques, and (under the influence of the flourishing environmentalist movement) attempted to employ the findings of physics to produce architectural solutions. Meanwhile, another group reacting to the pressure of social problems wished to approach architecture through dialectics.

Architects became more sensitive to social problems because of their increasing numbers and the erosion of their socio-economic status. In the 1950-1960 period, architecture had been one of the most sought after professions. The private sector recognized that this demand could be a potential source of profit. Prohibition of private higher educational institutions by the 1961 Constitution notwithstanding, permission was given for the establishment of several private schools. Large numbers of architects graduating from these schools inundated the profession. The Chamber of Architects tried to safeguard its monopoly and appealed to the Constitutional Court to rescind the legitimacy of private higher education. Although the regulation limiting architectural education to a state system alone was found to be legitimate, the decision did not result in the elimination of private schools already established; instead those schools were simply nationalized. The number of architects, in the thousands in 1960, grew to the tens of thousands in 1980.

The increase in the number of architects also created a differentiation within the structure of the professional body. Previously, architects working privately and in the public sector had maintained a privileged status and constituted a homogeneous group in terms of both skill and income, and therefore had easily unified around a professional ethos. The post-1960 body of architects, however, was considerably differentiated in terms of skill and social status. The number of commissions did not keep up with the increase in the number of architects, and the scarcity of opportunity, particularly for new architects entering the profession, intensified competition. In this situation, it was not possible for architects to unite as a group. Contradictory opinions held among different groups of architects also affected the Chamber of Architects. The Chamber came to represent the disadvantaged majority of architects and was dominated by socialist orientations; it stood in opposition to the orientation of successful practitioners.

Another phenomenon influencing architectural practice after 1960 was rapid industrialization. First building materials industries for the domestic market were established. These industries were not aimed at solving or rationalizing the housing problem in Turkey; their object was the middle- and upper-class housing produced by contractors. Rather than

rationalizing building, these industries were encouraging tendencies for showy consumption, and some of the architects became salesmen for these industries.

Fig. 6 Tekeli and Sisa, Lassa Tire Factory, Izmit, 1975-1977.

Industrial buildings also constituted a significant area of practice. Industrial monopolies, operating at high margins of profit, began commissioning aesthetically conscious industrial buildings (Fig. 6). This development was followed by the concentration of capital in large holdings. In the channeling of architectural practice in Turkey, holdings and banks had become more prominent than government as clients. The competitions organized by the Ministry of Public Works lost their preeminent roles. In addition, industrial buildings with aesthetic pretentions were commissioned by industrial monopolies when they were turned into holding companies. They then commissioned equally elaborate office buildings. Thus, the private sector now came into its own: contracts from the private sector were more profitable and much less of a risk to architects, whereas those from the government were inefficiently and inflexibly administered. Even after the economic crisis of 1978, architects were still actively employed by some parts of the private sector, particularly by the construction branches of large holding companies active in the Middle East.

Meanwhile, the processes of squatter building and build-and-sell continued at increasing rates and shaped the environment with an almost total exclusion of architects. The commercial development spread to all urban centers of Turkey, erased all regional differences and created a country-wide monotonous building texture. This texture exhibits no difference in Urfa, Samsun, Ankara, or Istanbul. The values of the consumer society, propagated by mass media, have created monotony. This monotony is the repetition of a few designs made by architects, each of whom was ironically educated to be a symbol of creativity.

The build-and-sell process lost its momentum with the economic depression of the late 1970s and the anti-inflationary policies since 1980 squeezed small contractors out of the market. It is now big capital which is ready to invest in housing for the middle classes. And it will be big capital which will have a key role in the shaping of the built environment.

In today's Turkey, where control of the economy has largely passed to corporations and holding companies, where the consumer values of Western societies predominate, and where the architectural profession increases in numbers and social differentiation, it is hardly likely that a coherent and unified architectural movement will emerge. Successful designers in private practice will be the ones commissioned by large corporations for in-country and foreign projects. They will be able to respond to these demands with the latest, most current in architecture. Their success will depend on their close connection to and participation in international style and fashion. Those architects who do not have access to these commissions will have to fall back on commercial developments in construction industry, with little opportunity to digress from set types which sell well and have become characteristic of all middle-class residential design.

Faculty members in architectural schools no longer have the practical experience in building that their predecessors had in the 1940s and 1950s. Isolated from practice, they have concentrated their energies on architectural theory, criticism, and history. This pursuit of scientific bases is not much different from the earlier approaches to international architectural currents: it essentially reflects a desire not to fall back behind developments in the West.

Since the 1960s, there has been a growing reevaluation of the role and status of the architect, particularly on the part of those who did not or would not participate in mainstream architecture. It was becoming quite apparent that, if the architect was to contribute to the formation of the built environment and to be of service to the majority of the population, the entire universe of building, its institutions and practices, had to be transformed dramatically. This consciousness of social responsibility on the part of the architect developed into a school of thought. Though calling for more equitable solutions, it could not develop and implement new strategies for building nor new design principles and processes, largely because of its limited access to political executive power. Some small beginnings were made in cases where architects of this persuasion were able, through alliances with other groups, to gain access to power. Between 1973 and 1980, when some social democratic mayors were elected, new planning and design strategies were launched to ameliorate the living conditions of disadvantaged groups and user participation was applied in the design of housing and new subsidized developments. However, such fresh initiatives remained isolated and could not develop into a socially conscious movement with a clearly articulated ideology.

While the left was not successful in establishing a single school of approach to these problems and remained fragmented, the right did not seem to concern itself with questions of the environment or of a national architecture and preferred to operate on a commercial basis alone. There was no attempt to define and nurture a national style. The only intervention from conservative circles seems to have been in the question of mosque design. They succeeded in supplanting the initial modernistic design of the Kocatepe Mosque in Ankara with a copy of an Ottoman mosque. On the whole, for them the built environment was shaped by consumerism alone.

A GENERAL EVALUATION

To sum up, a pre-industrial society such as Turkey, while being integrated into the world economic system, undergoes diverse transformations simultaneously. During these transformations, it has to be a nation on the one hand, and it has to be a part of the international system on the other. Yet it also has to create a national identity by defining cultural values that are distinctly its own.

In pre-Republican Turkey, Ziya Gökalp's dualist cultural theory admitted the coexistence of Turkish national culture and Western civilization. In Republican Turkey, Atatürk's monist theory removed the distinction between the two. Later, discussions for the resolution of the conflict could be discerned in attitudes which sought a fuller market integration with the world economic system without making any special attempts to exclude the cultural impact that came with it.

At this point, we arrive at a question which cannot be answered in terms of the Turkish experiment alone: are these three responses in opposition to each other? Or are they evolutionary stages of development? These questions cannot be answered without comparative data from other countries. For the time being, I am inclined to take them as three successive stages.

If we accept the validity of such a hypothesis, we can assert that a country entering the capitalist system will, in the early stages of its evolution as a nation-state, fluctuate between national and international architectural currents, and ultimately that international architectural currents will predominate. Within these fluctuations, it can be said that national architectural currents will be favored under authoritarian regimes with closed economies. But like nationalism itself, the idea of a national architectural movement can also be imported. However, it would be incorrect to look upon the adoption of foreign architectural models as mere acts of imitation. In each process of adoption not only were the basic tenets of each movement reinterpreted but also the validity of its solutions for the particular problems of the country was examined. In the case of Turkey, the reinterpretation of such movements was determined more by the ideological orientation of successive regimes than by the internal dynamics of the architectural profession alone. In peripheral countries, political movements can shape architecture when government has total control over building.

In this essay, the development of contemporary Turkish architecture was examined with a view to generate a theoretical framework for contemporary architecture process in peripheral countries. This framework can only be validated by similar analyses in other countries.

NOTES

1. Y.H. Bayur, *Türk Devletinin Dış Siyasası* (Foreign Policy of the Turkish State) (Istanbul 1942), p. 152.
2. H.E. Adıvar, *Türkiye'de Şark, Garp ve Amerikan Tesirleri* (Eastern, Western and

American Influences in Turkey) (Istanbul, 1956), pp. 135-136.

3. Y. Yavuz, "Cumhuriyet Dönemi Ankara'sında Mimari Biçim Endişesi" (Concern with Architectural Form in Republican Ankara), *Mimarlık* 11-12 (November-December, 1973), pp. 26-31.

4. S.H. Eldem, "Elli Yıllık Cumhuriyet Mimarlığı" (Fifty Years of Republican Architecture), *Mimarlık* 11-12 (November-December, 1973), p. 5.

5. *Ibid.*, p. 6.

6. Ç. Uluçay and E. Kartekin, *Yüksek Mühendis Okulu* (The Engineering School) (Istanbul, 1958), p. 130.

7. Y. Yavuz, *Mimar Kemalettin ve Birinci Ulusal Mimarlık Dönemi* (Kemalettin and the First National Architectural Period) (Ankara, 1981), p. 14.

8. S. Özkan, "Mimar Vedat Tek, 1873-1942," *Mimarlık* 11-12 (November-December, 1973), pp. 45-46.

9. Yavuz, "Cumhuriyet Dönemi," p. 17.

10. T.Z. Tunaya, *Türkiye'nin Siyasi Hayatında Batılılaşma Hareketleri* (Westernization Movements in Turkish Political Life) (Istanbul, 1960), pp. 86-92.

11. Z. Gökalp, *Türkleşmek, İslâmlaşmak, Muasırlaşmak* (Turkicization, Islamicization and Modernization) (Istanbul, 1918).

12. I. Aslanoğlu, *Erken Cumhuriyet Dönemi Mimarlığı* (Early Republican Architecture), Ph.D. diss., M.E.T.U., (Ankara, 1980), p. 17.

13. Quoted in S. Ural, "Türkiye'nin Sosyal Ekonomisi ve Mimarlık, 1923-1960" (Turkey's Social Economy and Architecture: 1923-1960), *Mimarlık* 1-2 (January-February, 1974), p. 24.

14. I. Tekeli, "Türkiye'de Kent Planlamasının Tarihsel Kökleri" (Historical Background of City Planning in Turkey) in T. Gök, ed., *Türkiye'de İmar Planlaması* (Reconstruction Planning in Turkey) (Ankara, 1980), pp. 52-53.

15. M. Sözen and M. Tapan, *50 Yıllın Türk Mimarisi* (Fifty Years of Turkish Architecture) (Istanbul, 1973), pp. 185-196.

16. Eldem, "Elli Yıllık," p. 6.

17. I. Aslanoğlu, *Erken Cumhuriyet Dönemi*, p. 17.

18. *Ibid.*, p. 35.

19. Ural, "Sosyal Ekonomi," pp. 34-35.

20. "Sergi Binası Müsabakası" (Competition for the Exhibition Hall), *Mimar* 5 (May, 1933), pp. 131-135.

21. A. Nijat, "Gazi Abidesi, Bursa" (The Gazi Monument, Bursa), *Mimar* 1 (January, 1932), pp. 4-5; "Yıldız Sarayı Tefriş Projesi" (Refurbishing the Yıldız Palace), *Mimar* 1 (January, 1934), pp. 8-11.

22. Ural, "Sosyal Ekonomi," p. 28.

23. N. Widmann, *Atatürk Üniversite Reformu* (Atatürk's University Reforms), A. Kazancıgil and S. Bozkurt, trs. (Istanbul, 1981).

24. F. Yavuz, *Ankara'nın İmarı ve Şehirciliğimiz* (City Planning and Ankara's Reconstruction) (Ankara, 1952).

25. I. Tekeli and I. Ortaylı, *Türkiye'de Belediyeciliğin Evrimi* (Development of Municipal Order in Turkey) (Ankara, 1978).

26. See, e.g. F.R. Atay, *Moskova-Roma* (Istanbul, 1932) and a series of editorials by Y.K. Karaosmanoğlu appearing under the title "Kadro" in *Kadro* during the 1930s.

27. Ü. Alsaç, "Türk Mimarlık Düşüncesinin Cumhuriyet Devrindeki Evrimi" (Development of Architectural Thought in Turkey during the Republican Period), *Mimarlık* 11-12 (November-December, 1973), p. 15.

28. Aslanoğlu, *Erken Cumhuriyet Dönemi*, p. 47.

29. B. Özer, *Rejyonalizm, Üniversalizm ve Çağdaş Mimarimiz Üzerine Bir Deneme* (An Essay on Regionalism, Universalism and Our Contemporary Architecture) (Istanbul, 1964), pp. 64-65.

30. Ural, "Sosyal Ekonomi," p. 29.

31. G. Oelsner, "Yaşayış Şekillerini Kuvvetlendirmek Lüzumludur" (Necessity of Ordering Living Patterns), *Arkitekt* 5-6 (May-June, 1946), p. 131.

32. See, e.g. Bedri Uçar's views as conveyed by Ural, "Sosyal Ekonomi," p. 32.

33. *Ibid.*, p. 43.

34. *Ibid.*, pp. 43-44.

35. *Ibid.*, p. 30.

36. *Ibid.*, pp. 36-37.
37. Özer, *Rejyonalizm*, pp. 74-75.
38. *Ibid.*, pp. 76-77.
39. E. Kortan, *Türkiye'de Mimarlık Hareketleri ve Eleştirisi, 1950-1960* (Architectural Movements in Turkey and Their Criticism: 1950-1960) (Ankara, 1971).

CHAPTER II

THE FINAL YEARS OF THE OTTOMAN EMPIRE

Yıldırım Yavuz and Suha Özkan

An understanding of the last hundred years of the Ottomans is vital for gaining a true perspective on modern Turkish architecture, and the social, political, and cultural context in which it developed. This turbulent century, known as the period of Ottoman Westernization, propelled Ottoman society through a series of social and cultural transformations which resulted in the emergence of modern Turkey.

The Ottoman discovery of Europe as a force to be contended with can be dated from the Treaty of Karlowitz (1699) following the defeat at Vienna. It was from this moment that attempts were made to investigate the causes of European military superiority and to introduce reforms based on European models. In 1721, an ambassador was sent to Paris to "make a thorough study of the means of civilization and education, and report on those capable of application."[1] Together with his report, the ambassador brought back with him a plan of the Fontainebleau Palace. The same decade witnessed a fleeting interest among Ottoman court circles in French manners, furniture, decoration and gardens. Notwithstanding these early interests, more continuous contact with European products and customs did not truly begin until the reign of Selim III (1789-1807) and the establishment of permanent embassies in Europe. Within the Empire, the most significant event was the establishment of a new army corps organized along European (French) lines called the New Order (Nizam-ı Cedid). It was for this new corps that a new type of building, military barracks in the European style, was introduced. The Ottoman reform movements were given further impetus by Mahmut II (1808-1839), who streamlined the bureaucracy, especially the Foreign Ministry, and re-established the new army corps, abolishing the Janissaries. It was, however, a decree promulgated in 1839 which more fundamentally reorganized Ottoman society. Known as the Tanzimat, the reforms granted equality under law for all subjects, changed the structure of administration, established a new judicial process and, more importantly, led to the founding of secondary and professional schools with European curricula. With the new educated elite, European literary forms were adopted, and the piano, along with Western style paintings and furniture, found its way into their homes.

The intellectuals of the Tanzimat period searched for a synthesis of political ideas and the Ottoman system of government. For example, they utilized the precepts of Islam to legitimize constitutional monarchy.[2] It would be up to the subsequent generations to look at the European systems of government as the only viable models. As the Empire began to lose territory and disintegrate, particularly following the Russo-Turkish war of 1877-1878, all intellectual energies were focused on formulating programs and ideologies which could provide the means to save it. Pan-Ottomanism, pan-Islamism and nationalism were proposed in turn, the latter in partial reaction to the formation of nation states in the Balkans. Turkish nationalism, which evolved out of pan-Ottomanism, had been reinforced by pan-Turkism, which stressed cultural and linguistic unity. The Western-educated Ottoman middle classes supported the nationalist program formulated after 1908 which became the blueprint for the Turkish Republic established in 1923. The emergence of a new political, social and cultural identity led to the development of new trends and styles in architecture.

During the earlier part of the nineteenth century, the most obvious European influences, besides those in military and technical matters, could be observed in life patterns and architecture. The Neoclassical style that prevailed in the West became popular in Istanbul for large buildings such as military barracks and palaces. It was introduced by various European architects and military engineers who had been recruited to design the edifices required for the New Order. Meanwhile, the members of the Imperial Guild of Ottoman Architects, trained to build for the simpler functions of traditional Ottoman society, lost their jobs to foreign and minority architects who, with their European training, were better equipped to cope with the complex spatial demands of the reforming sultans. Court architects were chosen from among Armenians (a notable example being the several generations of the Balyan family), or they were directly recruited from Europe. The art of building became a popular profession, especially among the Christian subjects trained abroad. Thus the nineteenth century witnessed the gradual decline of the traditional Turkish architect and a break in the evolution of traditional architecture.

Initial attempts at training the Ottoman architects in contemporary building techniques and European styles were made in 1801, at the new Imperial College of Military Engineering.[3] But a full curriculum of architectural education was established only with the opening of the School of Fine Arts (Mekteb-i Sanayi-i Nefise), in 1882. The majority of the teaching staff of this new school, which was modeled after the Ecole Nationale des Beaux Arts of Paris, consisted of foreign instructors, from France in particular. Thus, during the last quarter of the nineteenth century, the new School of Fine Arts in Istanbul had become a center for disseminating French taste and ideas in arts and architecture. On the other hand, the School of Civil Engineering (Hendese-i Mülkiye Mektebi), which had been organized in 1884 as an extension of the Imperial College of Military Engineering (Mühendishane-i Berr-i Hümayun), came under

German influence since many of its instructors were recruited from Germany and Austria. This was the period when Istanbul, a city of unique character with sober monuments, endless mazes of narrow streets and well-proportioned timber houses, was transformed into an arena of economic and cultural competition between France and Germany.

One of the more influential architects of the period was Professor Jachmund, who was sent to Istanbul by the Imperial German government to study the history of Ottoman architecture. He was employed at the new School of Civil Engineering as an instructor, and was officially appointed to design and build the Sirkeci Railroad Terminal, which was completed in 1890 (Fig. 7). This curious building with its horseshoe arches, large rose windows, minaret-like clock towers and profusely carved cornices, was a perfect example of oriental eclecticism that prevailed in the city at the turn of the century. It was an ill-bred style followed by foreign architects working for the Ottoman government who were quite ignorant of the Ottoman and Islamic architectural tradition. Notwithstanding its aesthetic drawbacks and its theoretical failures, the Sirkeci Railroad Terminal was still enthusiastically received by the Ottoman elite as a gateway to Europe and to modernity.

Despite his well-intentioned efforts to achieve harmony with the historic city in the design of the Sirkeci Railroad Terminal, Jachmund did not shy away from executing the Deutsche Orient Bank in a ponderous central European style (Fig. 8). This effective building, with its bulky, neo-renaissance mass in gray stone and its massive polygonal corner tower covered with a hemispherical copper dome, still stands as a witness to the German expansionist ambitions of the late nineteenth century.

Fig. 7 Jachmund, Sirkeci Railroad Terminal, Istanbul, 1890. General view from the north.

Fig. 8 Jachmund, Deutsche Orient Bank (Germania Hanı), Bahçekapı, Istanbul. View from the north.

Fig. 9 Vallaury, The Ottoman Bank, Karaköy, Istanbul. View from the northeast.

Vaullaury

F

A................tion (Düyun-i Umumiye Idaresi), Istanbul, 1899. View from the northwest.

Similar contradictions were observed in the work of the French architects who were working in the Ottoman capital during this period. Alexandre Vallaury, the chief instructor at the School of Fine Arts and Imperial architect for the palace, designed a highly ornate neo-renaissance facade for the Ottoman Bank (Fig. 9) which he built in Galata, the part of the city across the Golden Horn where the Europeans preferred to live and which had always been under foreign influence. It could be considered a most suitable facade for this monumental building, home of the institution which provided sorely needed French and British credit and which further impoverished the Empire.

On the other hand, the new headquarters of the Ottoman Public Debt Administration (Düyun-i Umumiye Idaresi), an institution run by European bankers, controlling the economic resources of the bankrupt Ottoman government, was carefully styled in pseudo-Islamic style (Fig. 10). It was situated on a hill in the historic peninsula with a commanding view of the busy port and was surrounded by many historic monuments. Completed in 1899, it was unquestionably the most glorious representative of oriental eclecticism with its huge, neo-renaissance mass, overlaid by elements of Eastern origin such as pointed arches, wooden grills and wide, undulating eaves (Fig. 11). A rich, exotic atmosphere was achieved in the interior with turquoise tile wall panels and fine veneering, while an unusual but striking variation of a traditional bath-house dome, studded with little round windows, was placed over the ostentatious entrance hall. The corbelled timber dome of the octagonal library tower was also a new interpretation of the traditional Islamic superstructure (Fig. 12). Nevertheless, despite Vallaury's efforts to achieve harmony with the environment, the sheer size and eclectic design of the building simply failed to fit the well-tempered silhouette of the Ottoman capital.

A further example of a similar type of building designed by Vallaury was the Imperial College of Military Medicine (Mekteb-i Şahane-i Tıbbiye), Haydarpaşa, on the Anatolian side of the Bosporus (Fig. 13). Completed in 1903, this immense school and hospital complex, reminiscent of military barracks with a large central courtyard, was also treated in an orientalizing eclectic style, with variously shaped arches, minaret-like clock towers and

Fig. 11 Vallaury, Ottoman Public Debt Administration (Düyun-i Umumiye Idaresi), Istanbul, 1899. Main entrance.

Fig. 12 Vallaury, Ottoman Public Debt Administration (Düyun-i Umumiye Idaresi), Istanbul, 1899. Interior of the octagonal library tower.

Fig. 13 Vallaury, Imperial College of Military Medicine (Mekteb-i Tıbbiye-i Şahane), Istanbul, 1903. General view from the west.

wide, undulating eaves, all juxtaposed against a huge, neo-renaissance mass. In contrast to the exterior details, the interior of the building was lavishly decorated in a baroque manner, as can be observed in the main entrance hall where a finely executed cast-iron stairway stands out. With its majestic rear elevation overlooking the historic peninsula across the sea and its serene backdrop of tall, dark green cypress trees, the building immediately draws attention to the entrance to the Bosporus, only to disappoint the observer with its oversized construction and naive styling.

Considering his efforts to achieve environmental harmony when building in historical quarters elsewhere, Vallaury was curiously reluctant to do so when he designed the Archaeological Museum which was built on the Topkapı Palace grounds, the fifteenth-century pavillion opposite Çinili Köşk (Fig. 14). This long, two-storey, U-shaped building was built in three different phases between 1891 and 1907. It was designed in an imposing Neoclassical style, with entrance porticos in the Corinthian order, surmounted by triangular pediments. This austere style was most probably dictated by what was being exhibited inside: the unique collection of Greco-Roman art excavated in every corner of the Empire. Nevertheless, the somber building with its gray, cut-stone exterior appears to be out of context with the sparkling delicacy of the Çinili Köşk nearby and the colorful splendor of the vast palace beyond.

Among other foreign architects working in Istanbul at the turn of the century was the Italian art-nouveau master Raimondo d'Aronco, who built several pavillions of the new Yıldız Palace and a large number of private timber houses on the Bosporus. Philippe Bello generally worked in collaboration with Vallaury. Otto Ritter and Helmuth Cuno built in an impressive Bavarian style in 1908 the Haydarpaşa Railroad Terminal. But it was mainly Vallaury and Jachmund who set the tone for the new imperial architecture of the Ottoman capital. Because of their influential academic positions, they were able to inculcate young architects with their own aesthetic norms. Turkish members of the student body, who were affected by the emerging Turkish nationalism and were opposed to the European domination in the architectural field, resented their influence.

Fig. 14 Vallaury, Archaeological Museum, Istanbul, 1891-1907. General view from northwest.

The reaction by the students marked the beginning of a trend in architectural styling, known as the First National Style (Birinci Ulusal Mimari), which dominated the next two decades under the leadership of two young architects, Vedat [Tek] and Kemalettin Bey.

Born in 1873 in Istanbul, Vedat [Tek] is known as the first Turkish architect with formal education in architecture. After completing his secondary education at the Ecole Nonge in Paris, he attended the Academie Julien for a career in painting and later the Ecole Centrale to become a civil engineer, but decided to become an architect instead. He completed his higher education at the Ecole Nationale des Beaux Arts in 1897. Upon his return to Istanbul in 1899, he was employed at the Municipality and became the first Turk to teach architectural history at the School of Fine Arts in 1900[4]. His French-based education did not lead him to impose a Beaux Arts style on his work and did not hinder him from seeking a more local, Turkish idiom. In the creation of this style, he was undoubtedly influenced by the ideas of the sociologist Ziya Gökalp, who formulated the basic principles of Turkish nationalism.

Vedat [Tek]'s first major work and probably his masterpiece, the Central Post Office in Istanbul, was completed in 1909 (Fig. 15). As one of the earlier manifestations of Turkish National architecture, the building displays the faults and merits of being a prototype. In spite of his efforts to dress the building with such Ottoman building elements as depressed or pointed arches in traditional proportions and with classical Turkish tiles applied to the spandrels, Vedat [Tek]'s European formation is still obvious in his shaping of the general mass and in his lavish use of tall, semi-circular pilasters with Corinthian capitals at the upper levels of the building. The large central hall with its iron and glass roof seems to have been inspired by

Fig. 15 Vedat [Tek], Central Post Office, Sirkeci, Istanbul, 1909. General view from northeast.

large banks or similar public buildings of the nineteenth century (Fig. 16). Nevertheless, the small masjid attached to the rear of the building is a fine example of the national style with its rich tile decoration on the exterior, its wide eaves and its curious little minaret (Fig. 17).

Vedat [Tek]'s Imperial Offices of the Land Registry (Defter-i Hakani), which was designed and built at the same time as the Central Post Office, display a more mature solution, with no architectural elements of foreign origin appearing on the facades (Fig. 18). Still, in spite of all the efforts of the architect to fit it into its immediate vicinity, this oversized building with its neo-renaissance mass composed in meticulous symmetry, rests awkwardly in its historical setting at the Hippodrome, facing the Blue Mosque.

Fig. 16 Vedat [Tek], Central Post Office, Sirkeci, Istanbul, 1909. Interior view of the main hall.

Fig. 17 Vedat [Tek], Central Post Office, Sirkeci, Istanbul, 1909. Attached mosque at the rear of the building.

Fig. 18 Vedat [Tek], Imperial Offices of Land Registry (Defter-i Hakani), Sultan Ahmet, Istanbul.

The architect's private residence which was built on a sloping, triangular corner lot in the fashionable Nişantaşı district was, by contrast, a small masterpiece of ingenious planning, which reminds one of early F.L. Wright houses, with its wide eaves and deep balcony canopies (Fig. 19). This four-storey building of asymmetrical design was placed on the difficult site in a masterful manner, with major interior spaces given an axial view of the street from the corner. Despite alterations of its ground and attic levels, the building still retains to a large extent its original character, at once reflecting the exquisite taste of its owner as well as strong nationalistic sentiments of those tempestuous years, through a rich display of tile decoration, finely proportioned arched windows, and a striking marble entrance (Fig. 20).

Kemalettin Bey, the second architect who developed the framework for nationalism in Turkish architecture, was born in 1870 to a family of modest means. He had his formal training at the new School of Civil Engineering, where he became an assistant to Jachmund, after graduating in 1891. Upon his return from Berlin in 1900, where he completed his post-graduate studies at the Charlottenburg Technische Hochschule, he was appointed as Chief Architect of the Ministry of War and simultaneously continued to teach at the School of Civil Engineering. Though he designed many houses and other public and private buildings during those years, his real opportunity to express his ideas on national architecture came only in 1909 when, at the age of forty, he was appointed as Chief Architect of the Ministry of Pious Foundations (Evkaf Nezareti), where he was entrusted with the management of a large technical office responsible for the restoration of historical monuments and the design of various new buildings. Restoration of the historical buildings of Istanbul gave Kemalettin Bey the opportunity to analyze the principles of Ottoman architecture and to formulate his own architectural idiom. Under his administration this office resembled a school of architecture, where experts trained under his guidance would disseminate his architectural views throughout the Empire.

It is known that, besides restoring many historical buildings, Kemalettin Bey created a large number of new buildings while working at the Ministry of Pious Foundations. Within a decade he built at least fourteen new mosques, nine mausolea, ten large office buildings, about forty school buildings and a variety of others such as prisons, hospitals and train stations.

His mosques are particularly noteworthy. The Ottoman mosque which, in the fourteenth century, had started as a modest prayer hall covered by an unpretentious dome, a simple entrance porch and an insignificant single minaret, developed to its majestic size during the glorious sixteenth century. But it began to degenerate with the decline of the Ottomans and reassumed its humble, primeval image in the final years of the Empire, when religion began to lose its influence in a society with drastically revised ethical codes. Kemalettin Bey's mosques are all interesting examples of religious architecture from this final period, designed as miniature but charming replicas of the early Ottoman mosque, endowed with the classical proportions of the sixteenth century. His small mosque at Bebek, skillfully placed among cypress trees on the edge of the Bosporus, is a fine

Fig. 19 Vedat [Tek], Private residence, Nişantaşı, Istanbul. View of the southwest corner.

Fig. 20 Vedat [Tek], Private residence, Nişantaşı, Istanbul. View of main facade.

Fig. 21 Kemalettin Bey, Bebek Mosque, Istanbul, 1913.

Fig. 22 Kemalettin Bey, Mosque of Kamer Hatun, Istanbul, 1912.

example of the architect's revivalist attempts at religious architecture (Fig. 21). Its plan, consisting of a square prayer hall, a triple bay entrance portico covered by small domes, and the single minaret attached to the western wall, closely follows the basic scheme of the early Ottoman mosque. However, the complicated superstructure with its four half domes, the octagonal lower dome pierced by windows, is a rather ingenious solution that gives the tiny edifice a stately and classic appearance from the exterior.

On the other hand, his mosque of Kamer Hatun, built in 1912 on an inconvenient lot squeezed between multi-storey rental blocks behind the British Embassy, reflects the cultural and aesthetic confusion that reigned in *fin-de-siècle* Istanbul (Fig. 22). The Beyoğlu district, where the mosque was built, had recently been transformed into a fashionable commercial and recreational center as an extension of the historic Pera (Galata). After the devastating fire of 1870, the whole region was built anew according to the new building and fire codes restricting even the minaret heights of the few mosques which were built in the district. The small mosque of Kamer Hatun, overpowered by multi-storey buildings, appears oppressed and miserable in spite of its richly decorated exterior. The mosque is entered from a small courtyard which is reached through a short tunnel on the ground level of the building. This unusual solution, though it contradicts the Ottoman building traditions, allows only the *qibla* of the mosque to be seen from the street. This wall is carefully outfitted with arched windows, tile inlays and a richly carved cornice, according to the precepts of the National Style. Juxtaposed against its towering neighbors, this small but ostentatious facade is symptomatic of the diminished role of religion among the cosmopolitan segments of Ottoman society.

Seven rental office blocks were planned by the Ministry of Pious Foundations to generate additional income. These seven buildings, only five of which were eventually completed, were all designed by Kemalettin Bey, and among them the Fourth Vakıf Hanı is generally considered to be his masterpiece (Fig. 23). This immense, seven-storey structure, built between 1912 and 1926 in the lively business district of Bahçekapı, is acclaimed for its well-ordered facade. It has a lavish display of rich geometric carvings, profiled mouldings, colored tile panels and a rich variation of window forms, all piled upon a basically well-balanced neo-renaissance elevation and represents the essence of the First National Style (Fig. 24). Behind the cut-stone facade, the building discloses a surprisingly sophisticated steel skeleton structure, randomly placed to extract maximum benefit from the irregular boundaries of the site. The protruding corner towers which enhance the symmetrical composition are covered by non-functional, pointed cupolas above the roof level, recalling the traditions of Ottoman architecture (Fig. 25). According to some historians, they were meant to conceal the elevator machinery when they were built, but this claim seems to be unfounded.[5] This last great edifice of the Ottoman period, with its majestic front elevation and plainly plastered rear facade, reminds one of a glittering stage set, laboriously propped up to recall the glorious past of a great empire.

Perhaps the most impressive and influential architectural achievement of Kemalettin Bey was his last building complex in Istanbul, which comprised a group of multi-storey dwellings specifically designed for low-income families who had suffered in the disastrous fire of 1918. This great fire, which took place during the last year of World War I, left behind more than three thousand smouldering buildings and added greatly to the housing shortage in the capital teeming with refugees from the Balkans. The Harikzedeĝan (Fire Victims) Apartments, as they have come to be known, were built during the difficult years of the War of Independence between 1919 and 1922 (Fig. 26). They were designed to shelter some 124 families in four different blocks of six storeys each and were built next to the eighteenth-century baroque mosque of Lâleli, at the corners of two intersecting streets. The apartments are also important because they are the earliest examples of reinforced concrete construction in the country. Each block was designed around a common, central courtyard, with four upper storeys reserved for apartments of varying sizes and the ground floors reserved for services and storage (Fig. 27). A series of twenty-five double-storey shops were placed on the ground level of the two front blocks, overlooking the main street, while each block was surmounted by a covered terrace for common use and laundry, which received natural light and ventilation from the central courtyards (Fig. 28). With their interesting, common courtyards encircled by open corridors on each level, their open stairs providing vertical circulation and, with their common laundry and service facilities, the buildings were obviously designed to accentuate social interaction, a notion alien to the introverted traditional Muslim family. Nevertheless, when completed in 1922, the apartments became extremely popular among the Turkish elite, who were willing to pay high rents for the meager comforts provided by these first high-rise housing blocks in the historic peninsula. The popularity of these

Fig. 23 Kemalettin Bey, Fourth Vakıf
Hanı, Istanbul, 1912-1926. Detail from the
southwest.

Fig. 25 Kemalettin Bey, Fourth Vakıf
Hanı, Istanbul, 1912-1926. Partial view of
southeast corner.

Fig. 24 Kemalettin Bey, Fourth Vakıf
Hanı, Istanbul, 1912-1926. Detail of
northwest tower.

Fig. 26 Kemalettin Bey, Harikzedegân (Fire Victims) Apartments, 1919-1922. General view.

Fig. 27 Kemalettin Bey, Harikzedegân (Fire Victims) Apartments, 1919-1922. View of a courtyard.

Fig. 28 Kemalettin Bey, Harikzedegân (Fire Victims) Apartments, 1919-1922. View of the attic.

apartments was concrete evidence of a changing life-style among the upper and middle classes.

Though definitely conceptualized through Western models, samples of which abound in many nineteenth-century European towns, the buildings were also admired for their general styling, in which the architect had tried to combine Ottoman imperial heritage with the contemporary ideas of a national architecture. The attic windows of the two front blocks were covered with undulating eaves echoing the baroque of the Lâleli Mosque next door. Though irrelevant to reinforced concrete construction, the ground shops and second-storey windows were outlined by segmental or semicircular arches, and the symmetrical layout was accentuated by projections common in Turkish civil architecture. The resultant eclecticism was in keeping with the general mood of the period, in which Turkish nationalism co-existed with European orientation yet in which internal forces of social cohesion were striving to overcome foreign domination and the effects of World War I.

NOTES

1. B. Lewis, *The Emergence of Modern Turkey* (London, 1961), pp. 45-46.

2. Ş. Mardin, *The Genesis of Young Ottoman Thought* (Princeton, 1962), p. 396.

3. M. Cezar, *Sanatta Batıya Açılış ve Osman Hamdi* (Osman Hamdi and the Western Orientation of Turkish Art) (Istanbul, 1971), pp. 62-63.

4. *Ibid.*, p. 552.

5. G. Goodwin, *A History of Ottoman Architecture* (London, 1971), p. 426.

CHAPTER III

FINDING A NATIONAL IDIOM: THE FIRST NATIONAL STYLE

Yıldırım Yavuz and Suha Özkan

On October 29, 1923, the Turkish Republic was proclaimed. There followed a series of reforms carried out by a group of dedicated nationalists headed by Mustafa Kemal Atatürk to build a nation-state on the ruins of the Ottoman Empire. An attempt was made to break all association with the past, and together with the abolition of the Caliphate in 1924, all members of the Ottoman dynasty were expelled from the country. The office of the *Şeyhülislâm* and the Ministry of Pious Foundations were abolished and replaced by departments of Religious Affairs and Religious Foundations under the Prime Ministry. Education, too, was secularized and centralized under the Ministry of National Education. In 1925, measures were taken to prohibit turbans and fezzes and to discourage the wearing of veils by women while Western-style clothing was adopted; in 1926, the Swiss Civil Code was adopted; and in 1928, the Arabic script was replaced by the Latin script. Western-oriented policies were pursued in the economic sphere as well. A free enterprise system supported by state capitalism was adopted at the Izmir Economic Congress of 1923 and was encouraged until the effects of the Great Depression dictated state intervention.

The most important event of the early 1920s which had lasting effects on the development of modern Turkish architecture was the declaration of Ankara as the new capital, replacing the imperial city of Istanbul, which was too closely associated with the Ottoman past. In 1923, Ankara, which had been the headquarters of the nationalist army during the War of Independence, was an insignificant central Anatolian town of some 20,000 people, with narrow, winding streets and simple mudbrick houses clustered around an impressive, ancient citadel on top of a steep hill. During the early years of the Republic, the face of Ankara was transformed by a vast building program whose aim was to adorn the new capital with monumental government buildings symbolizing the victory and ambitions of the new state.

The first edifice of this era was a single-storey, unpretentious building, begun in 1917 as a regional center for the then powerful Union and Progress Party (Fig. 29). Left unfinished because of the prolonged war and death of Hafi Bey, its young designer, the building was hastily completed in 1923 by the citizens of the city to be used as the first modest parliament of the new nation. Its wide wooden eaves, well-proportioned arched windows and symmetrical planning are hallmarks of the First National Style. Because of its small size and its inefficient layout, the building was soon turned over to the People's Republican Party.

Meanwhile, a partial city plan, composed of two different parts, was hastily prepared by Heussler in 1924, to give some direction to the growth of the capital. The first part of the plan called for the reconstruction of the old town, with a few roads and squares cutting into the existing urban texture, and for the development of the area between the commercial section and the train station as a government sector. The second part was designed to provide for housing for the hard-pressed government officials. More than 150 hectares of swamp land to the south of the railroad were designated for this purpose. The two-kilometer main artery from the station to the entrance of the citadel began to be developed in 1924 as the showcase of the Republic, with important buildings lining it on either side. Both parts of the plan served as the basis of a larger and more efficient city plan which was prepared by Hermann Jansen after 1928.

During its first year, the new capital was transformed into a large construction site with new buildings mushrooming everywhere. Yet, immediate financial shortfalls and acute shortages of trained architects and builders willing to work under difficult conditions impeded progress. Basic work was done by untrained and casual labor. Though haphazard

Fig. 29 Hafi Bey, Union and Progress Party Headquarters, later the first National Assembly, Ankara, 1917-1923.

work of this kind was accepted for the urgently needed housing out of sheer necessity, the design of official buildings requiring careful planning was a different matter. Vedat [Tek] was recruited from Istanbul to build the first two prominent buildings of the new capital, the new National Assembly and the Ankara Palas Hotel, located opposite to each other on the main artery.

The new National Assembly, completed in 1924, was designed as the headquarters of the People's Republican Party, but, as work progressed, it was found to be more suitable as a parliament. Partly because it was realized with a limited budget, the b   on its exterior, with its rubble walls built   ).
The two-storey, rectangular mass,   its longitudinal axis to the main street,   he center of one of its narrow sides.   as apparently necessitated by the axial ac   ll in the center of the building. As a resu   le faces a formally designed side-garden,   n on its central axis and, descending tov   l lily pond. Vedat [Tek] designed the bu   f meticulous symmetry, with parts pro   n order to enhance the symmetrical orgai   y of the entrance facade was surmount   e arched openings, to be used as a tribu   l relieving arches were placed over the r   while upper floor openings were bridg   arches with an occasional use of glazed   simple and restrained facades. Similarly   , geometric

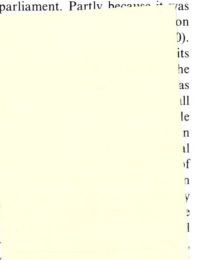

Fig. 30 Vedat [Tek], Headquarters of the People's Republican Party, later the second National Assembly, Ankara, 1926. Entrance facade.

Fig. 31 Vedat [Tek], Headquarters of the People's Republican Party, later the second National Assembly, Ankara, 1926. Assembly Hall.

arrays were laid in the tympana of the relieving arches, providing the coarse rubble stone walls with a certain degree of finish. The unpretentious building, the seat of the Turkish Republic for the next thirty years, had a simple plan with an ample but modestly furnished assembly hall surrounded by two storeys of offices (Fig. 31). But as early as the end of the 1930s, the building proved to be insufficient for the growing administration and the government announced an international competition to choose a new design for a third parliament building, inaugurated in the early 1950s and still in use today.

The only other building in Ankara with which Vedat [Tek] was associated was the Ankara Palas Hotel begun in 1924. Such a building was urgently needed in the new capital which lacked decent housing and proper hotels to serve visiting officials and dignitaries. The hotel was conveniently located in the immediate vicinity of the Assembly. After laying the foundations, Vedat [Tek] was compelled to return to Istanbul by the end of 1924, as a result of various disputes (Figs. 32, 33, 34). Kemalettin Bey, the other well-known architect of the First National Style, was then hastily recruited from Jerusalem where he had been officially appointed by the Arab Council to restore the Aqsa Mosque and the Dome of the Rock. He came to Ankara in 1925 and soon became the most influential architect in the capital. Despite his untimely death in 1927, his influence continued until the end of the decade and can be observed in the work of his friends, his disciples and few foreign architects who chose to design according to his principles of national architecture.

Kemalettin Bey's first commission in Ankara, where he was appointed as the Chief Architect of the General Directorate of Pious Foundations, was the design of a stately portal to the new Assembly building, which he framed with wide bands of profiled mouldings and an ornate cornice, somewhat damaging the integrity of the existing loggia. In the meantime, he worked on the plans of the interrupted Ankara Palas, which he designed as a two-storey, rectangular building with a great ballroom at the center,

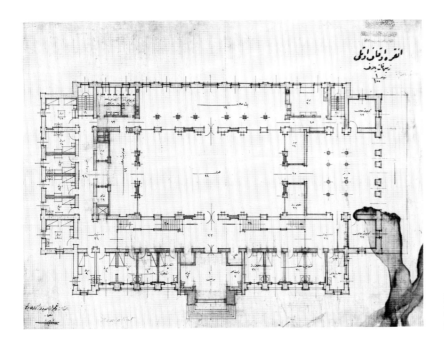

Fig. 32 Vedat [Tek] and Kemalettin Bey, Ankara Palas Hotel, 1924-1927. Original ground floor plan.

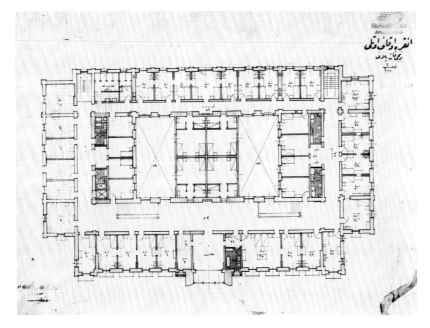

Fig. 33 Vedat [Tek] and Kemalettin Bey, Ankara Palas Hotel, 1924-1927. Original first floor plan.

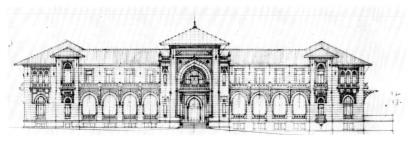

Fig. 34 Vedat [Tek] and Kemalettin Bey, Ankara Palas Hotel, 1924-1927. Earlier study for front elevations.

Fig. 35 Vedat [Tek] and Kemalettin Bey, Ankara Palas Hotel, 1924-1927. The great ballroom.

reminiscent of the historical Ottoman inns with central courtyards surrounded by guest rooms on two floors (Fig. 35). Besides the central ballroom, the ground floor was reserved for other public areas, such as the restaurant, the tea room and the administration office, while the guest rooms were placed on the first floor and the services in the basement.

When it was opened in 1927, the Ankara Palas was popularly acclaimed as the symbol of modernity and civilization, with its pressurized water and central heating systems, its Western type toilets and bathtubs and its powerful electric generator, a unique feature in this rural Anatolian town accustomed to dim kerosene lamps. For the next three decades it became the most popular gathering place in town, serving a glittering clientele composed of local and foreign diplomats engaged in political intrigues, high-ranking bureaucrats jockeying for positions, visiting statesmen with dubious missions and the Westernized nouveau-riche, who were eager to display their recently acquired taste in ballroom dancing, haute couture, and international cuisine.

In spite of all the modern services it offered to its guests, the building's facades were treated according to the principles of the First National Style, reflecting a nostalgia for Ottoman heritage (Fig. 36). The symmetrically arranged front elevation, a much admired feature at the time, was decorated with exquisite tiles, intricately carved marble balustrades, and ornate mouldings, cornices, and pediments. Although in an earlier sketch the facade shows a more coherent massing, it was later elaborated with more imposing corner towers and an oversized entrance portal, surmounted by a decorative wooden dome, a visual tribute to the traditional Ottoman cupola. In the early 1950s, when the central business district of the capital, along with the Assembly, moved further south past

the recently developed residential areas, the Ankara Palas, whose existence was so much dependent upon the proximity of an active parliament, was doomed to neglect and bankruptcy. Today, this graceful building stands closed in pitiful isolation, a faded memory of the early exciting years.

Fig. 36 Vedat [Tek] and Kemalettin Bey, Ankara Palas Hotel, 1924-1927. General view from the northeast.

During his last two years, Kemalettin Bey designed three multi-storey apartment blocks for government officials, several single houses and schools, and a large teachers' training college, his last great edifice, a building which marked the eclipse of the First National Style.

Of the three apartment blocks he designed, the one called the Second Vakıf Hanı stands out as the most interesting, with forty rental apartment units of various sizes, double-storey shops on the ground level, and a sizeable auditorium for the performing arts at its center (Figs. 37, 38). The seven-storey, reinforced concrete building was built on a trapezoidal lot about a hundred meters east of the Ankara Palas Hotel. It is apparent that the Second Vakıf Hanı was a variation of the Harikzedegân blocks; the central courtyard had been designed as a common circulation area and it enhanced social interaction among the residents. In the Second Vakıf Hanı, this central space was now occupied by a large auditorium. In general, there were fewer opportunities for contact and interaction in the newer project. Closed independent staircases, with separate entrances, served one part of apartments on each floor. Thus, people living under a single roof were total strangers to one another because of the flaws of the layout of this imposing and interesting building. The harsh climate of the city was partly responsible. For example, the attic, which had been designed as a common laundry and a children's play area, had to be closed off from the central court with large windows. Intimate relationship

Fig. 38 Kemalettin Bey, Second Vakıf
Apartments, Ankara, 1928. General view
from the southwest.

Fig. 37 Kemalettin Bey, Second Vakıf
Apartments, Ankara, 1928. Ground floor
plan.

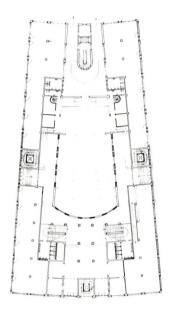

between the spaces of the attic and courtyard could not be maintained as
successfully as in the earlier Istanbul projects. Furthermore, framing the
ground floor shops with non-structural arches solely for the sake of visual
effect can also be considered a shortcoming in this reinforced concrete
building, which otherwise retains a well-balanced exterior composition
with protruding concave balconies and rounded corners. And yet, in spite
of its faults in planning and composition, the Second Vakıf Hanı was a
good example of high-standard housing with central heating, electricity,
elevators, and modern bathroom fixtures. It became the prototype for
multi-unit housing projects in the city, although none of these had its
spaciousness because they were usually built by commercial developers on
much smaller lots.

By the end of 1925, the tempo of the building activity in Ankara
quickened. Many new official buildings that required careful design were
commissioned. In addition to Vedat [Tek] and Kemalettin Bey, Arif
Hikmet Koyunoğlu, a disciple of Kemalettin Bey, and Giulio Mongeri, an
Italian who had been working in Turkey since before World War I, were
the pioneers chosen to design important public buildings.

During the late Empire, Mongeri was known as the designer of such
major buildings in Istanbul as the Karaköy Palas, a multi-storey office
building in neo-renaissance style with Byzantine features; the Maçka
Palas, a multi-storey apartment building continuing a nineteenth-century
eclecticism; and the new Italian Embassy in Maçka, a gigantic palace
ponderously styled and elaborately decorated. Though he was well-versed
in Byzantine architecture and made use of it in his designs when he worked
in Istanbul, he was also influenced by the prevailing National Movement
with which he had come into close contact while teaching at the Academy
of Fine Arts with Vedat [Tek]. By the time he was called to Ankara, he had

become sufficiently familiar with the principles of the Movement to be able to apply his personal variations to the imposing masses he had designed.

In Ankara, Mongeri was immediately entrusted with the task of designing the headquarters of the Agricultural Bank (Ziraat Bankası) and the newly established Turkish Business Bank (İş Bankası). The latter was conveniently located in the central business district, on a triangular corner lot (Fig. 39). The acute corner of the five-storey building, where the main entrance is placed, was rounded off to soften the visual effect, and this portion of the facade was composed with particular care, in order to accentuate the entrance axis. The building was ingeniously planned around a two-storey elliptical banking hall in a symmetrical manner (Fig. 40). The reinforced concrete structure, which made use of the traditional vault forms for the slabs, was hidden behind a thick facade of artificial stone that imitated the local stone of Ankara. The symmetrical facades, which reflect the influences of neo-renaissance styling, were fitted with building elements from the classical Ottoman period, such as pointed arches, wide eaves and carved mouldings, according to the principles of the

Fig. 39 Mongeri, İş Bankası Headquarters, Ankara, 1928. View of the main entrance facade.

Fig. 40 Mongeri, Iş Bankası Headquarters, Ankara, 1928. View of banking hall.

Fig. 41 Mongeri, Agricultural Bank, Ulus, Ankara, 1926-1929. General view.

Fig. 42 Mongeri, Agricultural Bank, Ulus, Ankara, 1926-1929. View of banking hall.

First National Movement. Particularly striking was the rich surface decoration, Mongeri's contribution to early Republican architecture. The spandrels of the window arches were filled with intricately designed arabesque carvings; the ground-floor windows were fitted with highly ornate bronze grilles; and the pilasters and columns of the upper storeys were crowned by elaborately carved capitals. The grand image befitted this bank which became one of the most powerful financial organizations in the country.

The second bank which Mongeri built in Ankara, the Agricultural Bank, was designed as an even more imposing edifice, built close to the central business district of Ulus, on a large site which faced the main avenue connecting the old town with the new districts to the south (Fig. 41). The five-storey, rectangular building was symmetrically planned around a central banking hall, with corners treated as square towers higher than the general roof level (Fig. 42). The reinforced concrete skeleton of the building was hidden behind a thick exterior wall, executed in finely cut, beige-colored stone, with the ones on the ground floor level carefully rusticated. Although the rear and side elevations were left untreated, the front elevation was richly embellished with every imaginable element of decoration used in contemporary Turkish architecture with the exception of wall tiles (Fig. 2). The windows were sharply framed by moulded architraves. The spandrels were covered with intricate carvings and rosettes like those of the Iş Bankası (Fig. 39). Geometric motifs were carved on the marble balustrades of the windows, and the wide eaves were gaily painted in polychrome patterns. The two-storey-high banking hall was also lavishly decorated with polychrome wall tiles, carved mouldings, and ornate balustrades.

With its huge, bastion-like corner towers and very tall storeys, the Agricultural Bank seems somewhat out of proportion with its immediate environment, particularly when compared with the General Directorate of the State Monopolies (Inhisarlar Idaresi), across the street (Fig. 43). This

Fig. 43 Mongeri, General Directorate of the State Monopolies (Inhisarlar Idaresi), Ankara, 1928. General view from the northwest.

small building, which also was designed by Mongeri, is a modest, charming example of the National Style of the late 1920s. The three-storey building was planned in an L-shaped form on a rectangular corner lot, with its corner treated as an octagonal tower capped by a lead-covered wooden cupola having wide wooden eaves as a brim. The simple layout consists of regular office rooms flanking the two central corridors that are hinged on the octagonal corner tower where the entrance hall and the stairs are placed for vertical circulation. In this otherwise simple building, the well-lit entrance hall with its marble floor, vaulted ceiling, and the spiraling staircase creates some spatial interest. The exterior of the reinforced concrete and brick structure, plastered over and incised with regular horizontal lines to imitate cut-stone construction, was sparingly decorated with ornaments commonly used in this period. The columns supporting the arches at the entrance and above the twin windows on the second floor level were surmounted by classical Ottoman capitals, while the spandrels of the arches and the few pediments placed above the roof level to enhance the symmetric organization were embossed with arabesques executed in gypsum. With its modest and well-balanced styling and its unpretentious scale, which fits so well into the urban texture of the old city, the General Directorate should be considered as one of the more successful representatives of the First National Style which otherwise had a penchant for unnecessary monumentalism.

The buildings designed by Arif Hikmet Koyunoğlu were all monumental with extravagant front elevations, usually hiding modest structures behind them. With its ostentatious facade, the Ministry of Foreign Affairs, now being used by the Ministry of Customs and State Monopolies, is typical of Koyunoğlu's monumentalism (Fig. 44). The two-storey rectangular building, completed in 1927, retains a simple, symmetrically organized plan of two floors of offices lining central corridors, a large entrance hall

Fig. 44 Koyunoğlu, Ministry of Foreign Affairs, later Ministry of Customs and State Monopolies, Ankara, 1927. General view from the west.

lined in marble and lit through the glass roof. Although the side and rear walls of brick were plastered, the cut-stone front facade was extravagantly decorated. To accentuate the symmetrical organization, the two ends and the central portion of the facade were projected outwards and lined with elegant white marble revetment. They were also surmounted by highly ornate pediments in several planes above the roof level, imitating marble roof gables. A triple-arched portico with an open terrace above it was placed in front of the entrance. The protrusions at the extremities were similarly composed with triple windows, their arches resting on engaged marble columns. This sumptuous front elevation was a most proper welcome for the eminent diplomatic visitors of the state when the building was being used by the Ministry of Foreign Affairs. Its insufficient size and modest interior, however, prompted the government to find a more suitable building for this ministry within a few years, and it was assigned to the Ministry of Customs and State Monopolies.

Another building which Koyunoğlu designed in the same manner was the Museum of Ethnography, a single-storey edifice with a palatial front facade that was built to house a rich collection of Anatolian folk art (Fig. 45). The Museum of Ethnography was organized and commissioned by Atatürk himself who saw it as the repository of folk art and culture, the base for his new cultural policy. The site for the museum was carefully chosen as well: a prominent hill halfway between old and new Ankara, as if this repository were meant to be the mediator between tradition and revolution. The symmetrical plan of the building consisted of large, rectangular halls arranged around a lofty central hall with a single dome, and a two-storey administrative wing in the back. The front halls at each end of the rectangular building were projected outwards to enhance the symmetrical organization. In front of the main entrance a triple-arched portico resting on four marble columns was reached by a long flight of

Fig. 45 Koyunoğlu, Museum of Ethnography, Ankara.

marble stairs. Set on a vast stone terrace with a bronze statue of Atatürk at its center, the cut-stone facade of the building was carefully decorated with white marble panels serving as window frames, ornate pediments placed above the projections and polychrome tiles laid in the tympana of the blind arches above the entrance doors. The visual quality of the building was further enriched by the use of ornate cornices around the edge of the roof and intricate bronze ornaments encircling the dome at its rim. Considered one of the finest monuments of the Republic, the building was chosen in 1938 as a temporary mausoleum for Atatürk, whose body was placed in a simple coffin below the central dome until his permanent mausoleum was completed in the early 1950s.

The last prominent building which Koyunoğlu designed in Ankara was the Turkish Hearth (Türk Ocağı) building located in the immediate vicinity of the Museum (Fig. 46). This national center for cultural activities contained, on its three floors, a large auditorium for lectures, seminars and performances; a specialized library on Turkish history and culture; classrooms for courses in painting, sculpture, arts, and crafts; meeting rooms; and halls for temporary exhibitions. It was in this center that some of the most important cultural programs were developed, under the close supervision of Atatürk himself, who wished to foster elements of European culture while concurrently developing specifically Turkish forms. The Turkish Historical Society and the Turkish Language Association founded by him were first located in this building before they were moved to their permanent homes. Its glittering auditorium was the site of international seminars and colloquia, as well as of local performances of such operas as *Madame Butterfly* and *Tosca*, sung in Turkish for the first time with all Turkish casts. With its weekly concerts, its matinees of poetry and contemporary drama and its courses and exhibitions of plastic arts,

the center became an enviable model for all provincial capitals.

For such an important and influential building, the architect had once again chosen the vocabulary of the First National Style so dependent on classical Ottoman forms. The building was planned symmetrically around the central auditorium, with all other activities surrounding it on two floors. The reinforced structure was once again enveloped by a thick, cut-stone wall on the exterior, and the front facade was sumptuously decorated with the usual ornamental elements. The resulting magnificence was perhaps aesthetically interesting, yet the choice of this specialized formal vocabulary, with its clear, and perhaps even nostalgic, associations with the Ottoman past, no longer found uncritical acceptance. For a center whose aim was to develop new forms of Turkish cultural life, the image of a discarded past was totally inappropriate.

The time had come for a drastic change in architectural direction and the axe fell on the last building of Kemalettin Bey. In late 1926, about ten months prior to his sudden death in July 1927, Kemalettin Bey was commissioned to design a teachers' training college. At the time, foreign buiding experts, coming particularly from Germany, were beginning to assume important consultative positions in the ministries. The architect had apparently been criticized by one of these experts stationed at the Ministry of Education for the ponderous style of his new design. The criticism started a heated dispute over the faults and merits of International versus National Style, involving local and foreign architects as well as officials and art critics. Aided by the effects of the 1929 economic crash, the internationalists, who were reluctant to spend an extra penny on useless decoration, won the argument. Turkish cities were now ready for the drab, prismatic forms of international architecture, so heavily influenced by the teachings of the Bauhaus school. Kemalettin Bey,

Fig. 47 Kemalettin Bey, Gazi Teachers' College, Ankara, 1926-1930. General view from the southeast.

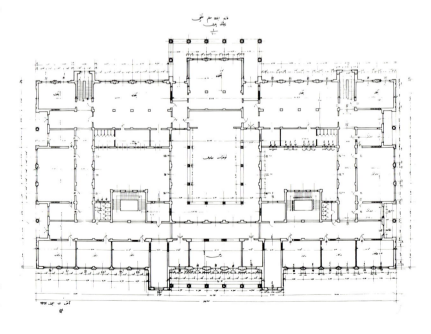

Fig. 48 Kemalettin Bey, Gazi Teachers' College, Ankara, 1926-1930. Original ground floor plan.

however, would not see the completion of his last building or the sudden expiration of the National Style, which he had so proudly initiated with Vedat [Tek].

The last great edifice of the First National Movement, the Gazi Teachers' Training College, was designed as a five-storey building on the outskirts of the capital (Fig. 47). It was planned symmetrically around a central auditorium for students, with classrooms, dormitories, laboratories, office rooms, and interior courts on several floors (Fig. 48). Although completely built in reinforced concrete, its walls were covered with cut-stone on the exterior, in keeping with the traditions of the National Style. Symmetrical planning was stressed on the facades, which had tower-like protrusions capped by independent gable roofs. The main entryway on the central axis was provided with an imposing, two-storey portico, divided into five equal bays and spanned by pointed arches on tall marble columns. The central axis was further emphasized by the small dome of the observatory, placed at the center, above the roof level. The central auditorium, in two storeys, with a U-shaped balcony resting on stout columns, is lit through the flanking inner courts (Fig. 49). Completed in 1930, this immense building, provided with all the comforts of a modern educational institution, has withstood the test of time and is still considered to be the main center for training teachers. Although similar institutions have since been built, none were built to the same construction standards. It is perhaps fitting that this building was the last example of the First National Movement. The search for a specific architectural identity would not be resumed until the beginning of World War II.

CHAPTER IV

TO BE MODERN: SEARCH FOR A REPUBLICAN ARCHITECTURE

Afife Batur

The period between 1930 and 1940 marks the formation of Republican architecture: it is in this period that its forms were developed and its functions ascertained. The building processes of the period, with their particular problems and distinctive design solutions were fundamentally affected by the historical conditions of the decade ushered in by the Great Depression.[1]

If the 1920s were characterized by upheavals and transformations with the abolition of the Ottoman political structure and the inauguration of Republican reforms, the 1930s were marked by the crystallization of Kemalist ideology and the consolidation of the new Turkish state. The initiatives of the 1920s, however, provided the Republican cadres with invaluable experience in building the entire infrastructure of modern Turkey. Networks such as railroads, ports, utilities and telephone companies were nationalized and major national banks were established. Yet, the state would not have control over the economy until the 1930s.

The Treaty of Lausanne (1924), which recognized the Turkish Republic, stipulated that customs duties remain at the 1916 levels until 1929. Moreover, no controls over currency and foreign exchange could be implemented. As a result, domestic industry could not be protected and hard currency reserves were spent on purchasing consumer goods from Europe. In 1927, for example, ninety percent of the imports were industrial products, only thirty percent of which were capital goods. These were years when "Turkey sold figs in exchange for tiles and wheat for ceramic wood-burning stoves."[2] These liberal economic policies began with the Izmir Economic Congress of 1923 and had to be abandoned with the coming of the Great Depression at the end of the decade. Customs duties were raised and in 1930 the Central Bank was established. Etatist policies came to be fully implemented by the time the first Five-Year Industrial Plan was put into effect in 1933. In the 1930s the consolidation of the reforms took place under an increasingly *dirigiste* system.

Whereas the Atatürk reforms introduced into the life of the nation such concepts and values as innovation, nationalism, functionalism, utilitarianism, objectivism, and a belief in science, technology and progress, it was the etatist economy which more directly influenced the architecture of the period since the public sector was responsible for almost all building activity other than residential construction. In fact, it could be said that the new economic policies had a major effect in shaping the built environment of the decade.

The building program as formulated in the early years of the Republic called for the reconstruction of the war-stricken Anatolian cities, the founding of a new capital, and the construction of bridges and railroads. This program was further developed in the 1930s. The priorities of the latter decade included developing the capital city, installing service and industrial buildings throughout the country, and generating models for school buildings. Above all, the energies of central and local authorities were spent on the construction of public works in the main cities and towns.

PUBLIC WORKS

Among the major goals of the new leadership was an orderly human environment, in their eyes the hallmark of a contemporary society. Moreover, this image of the modern city had to compete with the lively cosmopolitan port cities of the Ottoman period, Istanbul, Izmir, Salonica, which still remained as models of urban life in Turkey.[3]

A series of laws enacted between 1930 and 1935 addressed the organization of urban entities. These included the Municipality Law (Belediye Kanunu no. 1580) of 1930; the Municipalities Bank Law (Belediyeler Bankası Kuruluş Kanunu no. 2031) of 1933; the Municipal Public Works Law (Belediyeler Yapı ve Yollar Kanunu no. 2290) of 1933; and the Municipalities Construction Board Law (Belediyeler İmar Heyeti Kuruluş Kanunu) of 1935. These laws were to serve adequately for a number of years though enacted at a time when construction activity and the rate of urbanization were limited. "Despite the amendments made later, it could be said that the framework established in this period determined the present-day functioning of municipalities."[4] Municipal services expanded and defined by these laws were turned over to municipal ownership and control, and the building of public works was begun. Limited resources notwithstanding, the necessary infrastructure for settlements with over 10,000 population was in place by the end of the decade.[5]

Providing some autonomy to municipalities, these laws established centralized control. As a result, despite differences in scale, all municipalities were uniform in program and practice. "An examination of these programs reveals that their fundamental purposes were to represent the Republican regime, to establish an urban life-style befitting 'a civilized country,' to improve public health, and to increase municipal revenues."[6]

A set of symbolic urban elements uniformly employed in the building or the reconstruction of all settlements consisted of the main street of the town (Gazi Bulvarı) leading to a Republic Square, in the middle of which would stand a statue of Atatürk. In small towns, this formula was realized with a bust of Atatürk placed in the middle of a symmetrically organized garden in front of the municipal building. Another symbolic structure was the municipal building itself. "Incentives were especially given to smaller municipalities to construct exemplary buildings, and pictures of such buildings were published in the *Municipalities' Journal.*"[7] The minimum building program for settlements also included an Atatürk primary school, a state office building, and a People's House (Halk Evi).

Although the construction of power and water systems was the main priority of the public works program, the provision of paved roads, sidewalks and green spaces was considered crucial for the creation of a contemporary image. The complaint of Lütfü Kırdar, then mayor of Istanbul, illustrated the necessity of these programs: "Even in Istanbul, there is nothing that could be called a street in the downtown districts." Mayors could now boast of their new tree-lined cobblestone streets with sidewalks. However, the Municipal Public Works Law stipulated the elimination of dead-end streets. This was carried out without any consideration of existing settlement patterns and was the beginning of the demise of the historical environment since major arteries began to cut through city centers. Although there was clearly an intention to create healthier cities, the doctrinaire and rigid implementations did not make for a more satisfactory urban morphology and texture; they only intruded with contemporaneity. The most positive undertakings of the period were the planning of urban green spaces including large parks and the establishment of plant nurseries. "The directives of the Republican leaders to install urban parks influenced not only big cities but also small towns which were still a part of the natural environment. Even in small towns, municipal gardens with fountains were laid out." [8]

Apart from Ankara, the most successful large-scale urban planning effort was that of Izmir. Izmir was of great significance to the Republic: the first bullet of the War of Independence was fired there and it was there that the war came to a close. A major effort at the reconstruction of the city was all the more necessary because it had been badly ruined by the Great Fire and depopulated at the end of the war. In addition, its heritage as a cosmopolitan port city during the Ottoman period and its commercial potential as Turkey's major export center assured its quick reconstruction.

The personalities of the mayors of Izmir also influenced the Republican reorganization of the city. Both Şükrü Kaya, later Minister of the Interior, and Dr. Behçet Uz, his successor, were committed to urban planning and to five-year working plans. Initially, efforts at rehabilitation of the ruined areas according to a partial master plan prepared by Henri Prost and Réné Danger were hampered by the lack of capital. At this juncture the personality and energy of Dr. Uz proved to be crucial. A medical doctor by training, he placed emphasis on public health and environmental issues, but was also a resourceful civic leader with a businessman's acumen. His way of generating the necessary capital was the establishment of Kültür Park, the site of the Izmir International Trade Fair. Originally envisaged as a thirty-three hectare area, the park expanded to forty-three hectares in three years. With its pavilions, green spaces, artificial lakes and botanical gardens, it introduced a totally new urban environment to Izmir. Not only did it become financially self-sufficient but was so commercially successful that it generated surplus funds for the city. In addition, as in the case of all other international fairs it became an architectural showcase for its participants and afforded Turkish architects the opportunity to encounter and experiment with the latest in architectural styles. Dr. Uz's implementations went far beyond the scope of the Prost-Danger plan and in 1938 a new master plan had to be proposed. The urban renewal of Izmir continued into the 1940s and surpassed all expectations.

THE FOUNDATION OF ANKARA

In 1919, "on the 27th day of December, an open military vehicle stopped at the top of the Dikmen hill with a bird's-eye view of Ankara beneath. Mustafa Kemal looked down. Those coming to meet him had formed a black line meandering across the desolate, snow-covered fields beginning from the next hill, down to the station and all the way to the Government House. The masses of people against the backdrop of the desolate, snowbound city nevertheless convinced Mustafa Kemal that there was a vital spirit here." [9] Four months later the National Assembly was established in the Government House and the War of Independence was conducted from there. The new government became known as the Ankara government. On October 13, 1923, sixteen days before the formal declaration of the Republican regime, Ankara was named the capital of the Turkish state. This decision was an official recognition of a *de facto* situation; in fact, Mustafa Kemal had said, "Ankara has become the center; occupying armies have never reached further than its outposts."[10]

Although it was centrally located and well connected to the railway network, it was the only city in Anatolia whose significance depended on its role in the War of Independence alone. Compared to cosmopolitan Istanbul or even to such alternatives as Konya, Kayseri and Sivas, the choice of Ankara provided a *tabula rasa* upon which a new order could be constructed. Common opinion of both native and foreign observers described it as "poor, malaria-ridden and waterless,"[11] "with narrow streets and flimsy wooden houses,"[12] and "unequalled in nastiness."[13] Thus, to fashion a capital city out of this Ankara "was itself a courageous act among all other acts of heroism leading to the rebirth of Anatolian Turkishness."[14]

The first steps in the development of Ankara were taken very soon after it had been declared the capital. The municipality was organized on February 16, 1924 and a 4,000-hectare area was expropriated through special legislation passed on March 16, 1926. The Emlâk ve Eytam Bankası was established to finance building activity and a large portion of its resources was allocated to the capital in the early years. Factories were founded to manufacture building materials (brick, tile, timber, etc.) and worker-housing was built. Efforts were made to plan and coordinate the building activity necessary to cope with a rise in population and with the functions of a capital city. The winner of the 1928 International Competition, the Jansen plan was approved for implementation on July 23, 1932. Despite speculative pressures it was, by and large, successfully implemented until 1938. The chaotic building boom of the late 1920s was now controlled. Instead of haphazard mushrooming of buildings, there was now an equally rapid but planned construction program. Jansen's plan approached urban development with a rationalist methodology. It was primarily concerned with developing and implementing macroforms,

71

the major axes, the open spaces, and zoning. Smaller forms such as individual neighborhoods were to be developed later as the lessons of the new developments were learned.

The plan consisted of the following principal decisions: the Atatürk Boulevard would be the north-south structural axis and would extend to Çankaya. The second axis would intersect the Boulevard at right angles in Ulus, connecting to the Istanbul road on the west, following the natural contour of the topography in the east, and then crossing the southern part of the old town. The new city was planned outside the confines of the old city around these axes. The old town was to be preserved. Its western section adjacent the new city was to be modernized. The commercial center was to remain in Ulus, but the new administrative district was to be placed in Yenişehir. The area surrounding the Atatürk Boulevard was arranged in a grid pattern for housing.

The development of Ankara could only be realized under very special circumstances. A decision was made to separate the new city from the old; areas to be developed were expropriated and turned over to an executive organization; a relatively autonomous Planning Directorate capable of effective action outside the usual bureaucratic channels was established; and a bank which could finance building activity was founded. Tekeli points out that such a consolidated pattern of action supported by political leadership is unique in the history of the Republic.[15] It is sufficient to cite just one figure to illustrate this point. In Ankara, municipal expenses per person were twenty-eight times that of the average for Turkey in 1927, and twenty-three times in 1931. Infrastructure expenses met from the central budget (electricity, water and gas installations) are not included in these figures.

While building activity was interrupted throughout the country by the impact of the Great Depression, it still continued in privileged Ankara. The development of Ankara has been a popular subject not only in professional literature but also in novels, memoirs and popular articles. The works of two seminal writers, Falih Rıfkı Atay and Yakup Kadri Karaosmanoğlu, allude to the problems of the building boom. Atay, for

Fig. 50 Akalın, Railroad Terminal, Ankara, 1937. Detail of interior.

example, lamenting the excesses of land speculation, stated that "local conditions have shattered hopes for the most advanced city in the world; such a city could no doubt have been achieved with a lesser outlay than has been spent thus far." Atay also said, "Mustafa Kemal has been able to establish an administration capable of implementing his reforms, but not one strong enough to implement a city plan."[16] Nevertheless, Atatürk's support of Jansen's plan and the fact that the former mayor of Izmir, Şükrü Kaya, was now the Minister of the Interior, insured the emergence of Ankara as a modern capital.

During the 1930s major projects were realized in the public sector. The needs of ministries, banks and other governmental agencies were met before the end of the decade. The cityscape took shape and urban planning standards, which would continue to be valid until the 1950s, were formulated.

Service and Industrial Buildings

Railroad construction was not considered merely as an infrastructure investment but, since it was closely associated with Prime Minister İnönü, it became a political symbol of the Republic. Through it new activities and buildings were introduced into Anatolian cities and towns. Railroad stations in particular were the first modern buildings in most centers (Fig. 50).

According to the first Five-Year Plan, factories were built throughout Anatolia. As a result, the share of industry in the gross national product rose from 11.4 percent to 18.8 percent by the end of the decade. Large factories, all built between 1934 and 1939, introduced a new building type into the architectural inventory of Anatolia[17] (Fig. 51). These enterprises were obviously more advanced than railroad stations in terms of modern functional design. The objective goal and the technology inherent in the design of these buildings brought with them a mode of thinking and influenced, albeit indirectly, the client (i.e. the government), the user, and the man on the street as well as the designer and the engineer. This influence is reflected in the press of the period.[18]

Fig. 51 Sümerbank Textile Plant, Nazilli, 1935-1937.

Fig. 52 Necmeddin, Gazi Primary
School (Gazi Ilk Mektebi), Izmir, 1934.

Educational Buildings

In the 1930s, when a national educational policy was established and schools were reorganized around modern secular educational principles, an average of fifty primary schools and twenty middle schools were opened annually. Each city or town strove to build its own Gazi School (Fig. 52). Symbolic quality was given priority over functionality in these buildings, and they came to symbolize the regime as much as other government buildings.

Housing

Although housing is discussed in detail in the last chapter of this book, several summary remarks should be made here. During the etatist economy of the 1930s the public sector was not involved in housing development except for isolated cooperatives, chiefly because funds were restricted and urban populations outside of Ankara were not growing at a rapid rate. Still, the fact that the administration had not articulated any strategies for housing meant that its cadres did not develop any expertise and therefore would not be able to meet future needs.

From the beginning Ankara confronted urbanization problems that would strain other Turkish cities later. Between 1927 and 1940 its annual population growth rate was six percent.[19] It was the unfulfilled demand for housing, high rents and spiralling land prices that became major handicaps in the development of Ankara.

Single-family housing and, to a much lesser extent, apartment blocks remained the favored form of the private sector. In fact, almost half of all the published designs and completed projects in the journal *Arkitekt* were residential buildings in Ankara and, to a lesser degree, in Istanbul.[20] Young Turkish architects excluded from large government projects which had been entrusted to foreign practitioners found a fruitful arena for professional activity in the residential construction of this period (Fig. 53).

Fig. 53 Denktaş, Tüten Apartments, Istanbul, 1936.

IDEOLOGY, EXPRESSION, SYMBOL, AND STYLE

The building program described above presents a list of investment and building activities directly dependent upon the etatist economy, and by its very nature represents official ideology. It must be stressed that the building activity of the decade, as compared to other periods, was more engaged. Its ideological engagement can be clearly discerned in the programs, priorities and fundamental motivations behind them.

A version of modern functionalism, which became the salient characteristic of the period, was adopted as the most appropriate medium of expression. The Ottoman Revivalist Style, otherwise known as the First National Architectural Movement, had been declared anachronistic and was abandoned. The orientation toward modern architecture was perceived as the prerequisite for modernization, and for attaining the transition from an Islamic-Eastern cultural basis to a Western one. This prevalent tendency, not yet elaborately formulated, was also reflected in the press. *Hakimiyet-i Milliye*, an influential newspaper, published the following on July 4, 1927, concerning the Ministry of Health (Fig. 54) which was under construction at the time:

> The Ministry Building has indeed become the most modern building of Ankara. It resembles the latest and most modern buildings of Europe. That the building is erected in Yenişehir has additional significance because in planning our Ankara, we had adopted the principle of constructing grand and monumental buildings in Yenişehir and along its backbone, the Gazi Bulvarı.[21]

The move toward modernism in architecture was quite radical; it was espoused on the highest levels of the administration with unanimity and was implemented at all levels of government with persistence. The clearly articulated goal of the Republic was to catch up with the material culture and technological advancement of the West.[22] It was natural therefore to call upon foreign experts. After hesitant beginnings in the early years of the Republic, broader utilization of outside expertise was called for in the wake of the Industrial Incentives Act of 1927 (Teşvik-i Sanayi Kanunu).[23] This law allowed not only the technical personnel required by industry, but also planners, engineers and architects to work in Turkey, thereby signalling the beginning of a new era. Fourteen architects and planners are known to have been officially invited to Turkey between the years 1927 and 1940.[24] Nine of these were German and one Austrian. This demonstrated that "strong cultural ties existed between the Early Republicans and the German-speaking sector of Europe."[25]

Fig. 54 Post, Ministry of Health (Sağlık Bakanlığı), Ankara, 1926-1927.

The presence of foreign architects is not the only explanation for the introduction of modern architecture to Turkey, its rapid acceptance and wide application. Modern architecture was also a response to certain cultural or technological requirements and conditions. There was a great demand for a range of specialized buildings from monumental public structures to factories or hospitals as well as for housing.

Yet the financial resources of the state were limited and the building industry and technology were backward. It was necessary both to develop a building industry and to change building procedures to ensure faster and cheaper construction. For instance, in 1924, Haydar Bey, the pragmatic mayor of Ankara, "... went to Europe along with his advisors.... Considering that Ankara needed construction before anything else, he put in his suitcase samples of the city's soil and stone; he showed these to experts in Europe and had them analyzed. He wanted to learn if cement, bricks and tile could be manufactured from them."[26] The transformation of building procedures is also described in an issue of *Hakimiyet-i Milliye*:

> Two kilometers beyond the old city ... rental properties are being constructed. In the formation of the first nucleus of Ankara, fantasy is avoided. Buildings are lined up along straight streets.... Mayor Haydar Bey has already said that the plan of the new city is that of Potsdam. The architecture of these one- or two-storey buildings was no different from that of similar housing projects in the West. It may be regretted that neither Turkish nor Byzantine style was adopted, but in such matters the opinion of architects was not solicited. The founders of new Ankara want simple and comfortable houses ... aesthetics are not given priority. This attitude represents a great deal of progress from the past ... the grills adored by Loti no longer decorate the windows of the new city. Modern hygiene demanding ample light and air ... has vanquished one of the oldest traditions.[27]

The so-called "Republican Bourgeoisie,"[28] consisting of military and civilian officials, played an important role in the acceptance of modern architecture. These highly-paid officials had found in modern architecture an appropriate response to their search for a new life-style: thoroughly contemporary, without a hint of the past. These qualities were decisive in the diffusion of modern architecture, particularly in residential architecture. Yakup Kadri Karaosmanoğlu, in his fictionalized memoirs *Ankara*, mentioned the appearance in 1926 of Cubist architecture and criticized a certain type of Republican bourgeoisie through a description of their houses:

> Among the villas extending from Yenişehir to Kavaklıdere it was impossible not to come across towerless, eaveless buildings. Thank God, this trend which spread during the incompetence and poor taste of early years, was *suddenly* [emphasis mine] replaced by Modern architecture.... They too used to live in a house with a tower and overhanging eaves. Later, like all the

Fig. 55 Holzmeister, Ministry of Defense (Millî Savunma Bakanlığı), Ankara, 1927-1931.

families, they also were affected by a consuming urge for the Modern. Hakkı Bey outdid everyone else in the matter of a house and displayed the first example of *the cubist* to everybody. Hakkı Bey's house became the first of the buildings with glazed corners, lacquered doors and ceilings hollowed out for concealed electrical installations.[29]

The villas of Çankaya, described by Yakup Kadri, no longer exist. Nevertheless, the first application of functionalist forms can be illustrated by some industrial buildings. As previously mentioned, industrial buildings along with other service buildings constitute both the material basis of the concept of modern functionalism and provide its early examples. One of the early buildings is the Ankara Textile Factory (later Yün-Iş) with its eaveless flat roof, white stucco walls, horizontal band windows and rectangular masses.[30] Another example is the Alpullu Sugar Factory, which started production in 1926.

Modern architecture began to replace Ottoman Revivalism in institutional buildings after 1927. The first significant building was the Ministry of Health (Fig. 54) by Theodor Post (1926-1927). It was followed in 1927-1931 by the Ministry of National Defense (Fig. 55) by Holzmeister. The modern trend was validated after Jansen won the competition for the Ankara Master Plan in 1928. Among the architects commissioned to design large-scale public buildings, Clemens Holzmeister and Ernst Egli were in the forefront.

Clemens Holzmeister (1886-1983) was assigned to plan the Administrative District designated in the Jansen Master Plan, and to design some of its buildings. Few architects in the world have ever been commissioned to design all administrative buildings of a capital city. Holzmeister's work, commencing in 1928, included, along with the general site plan, the Ministry of National Defense, the General Staff Building (Fig. 56), Presidential Palace (1930-1932), the Ministry of the Interior (Fig. 57), the General Directorate of Security and Gendarmerie (1932-1934), the Ministry of Public Works (1933-1934), the Court of Cassation (1933-1935), the Ministry of Commerce (1934-1935), as well as the Central Bank (1931-1933) and the Emlâk Kredi Bankası (1933-1934) outside the

Administrative District. The number, scale and nature of these commissions made Holzmeister the most powerful architect of the period. The most characteristic features of a Holzmeister design are rectangular plans with central courtyards or classical U-shaped schemes; symmetrical axial plans and elevation arrangements; and extended block units without joins. The massing and spatial organization recalls the classicism of Perret, "the last great representative of the French academic culture."[31] Although the building did not attain the same mastery and sensitivity, they connected Holzmeister's work to the preceding era. On the other hand, Holzmeister exhibited characteristics attributable to the Vienna School of the early Modern Movement. For example, the circular layout of corner volumes in the General Staff Building and the joining of these volumes through small projections to the main rectangular block are traits seen in the pioneering works of The Vienna School. The plasticity of the facade achieved by projections of an inverted T-form and the simple wall texture in the Officers' Club (Orduevi) (Fig. 58) and in the Ministry of Defense recall the Purism of Hoffman, particularly his Resthouse in Purkersdorf built in 1903. Contemporary building technology was employed in all these buildings. Yet, with his insistent use of classical schemes, axial arrangements, and his preference for stone as a building material, it is

Fig. 56 Holzmeister, General Staff (Genelkurmay Başkanlığı), Ankara, 1929-1930.

Fig. 57 Holzmeister, Ministry of the Interior (İçişleri Bakanlığı), Ankara, 1932-1934.

Fig. 58 Holzmeister, Officers' Club (Orduevi), Ankara, 1929-1933. Main block.

difficult to consider Holzmeister as a true representative of the Modern Movement. These characteristics, reinforced by the use of a colossal style of columns rising two or three storeys high in some of his buildings such as the Court of Cassation and the Grand National Assembly, indicate his proximity in the spirit to National Socialist architecture.

The Grand National Assembly (1938-1960) is the largest and most important work of Holzmeister. In the international architectural competition of January, 1937, three projects out of fourteen entries were presented to the government as worthy of the first prize and implementation.[32] Holzmeister's project was chosen, and the foundations were laid in October, 1937. The construction, interrupted by the war, could only be completed in 1960.[33] In spite of this postponement, the characteristics of the original design were implemented. Compared to the other two winning projects, it is simpler, less pretentious and clearly horizontal. Its monumentality does not appear overwhelming in the present cityscape of Ankara. It is also harmonious with the rest of the buildings in the administrative district.

The interior spatial arrangements of the Grand National Assembly immediately reveal Holzmeister's skill and craftsmanship. The auditorium used as the General Meeting Hall or as the Senate does not display a crude monumentality, despite its grand scale. For the architectural elements and

Fig. 59 Holzmeister, The Residence of
the President (Cumhurbaşkanlığı Köşkü),
Ankara, 1930-1932. General view.

Fig. 60 Holzmeister, The Residence of
the President (Cumhurbaşkanlığı Köşkü),
Ankara, 1930-1932. Plan of first and
second levels.

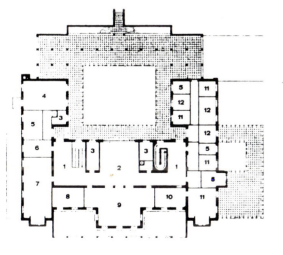

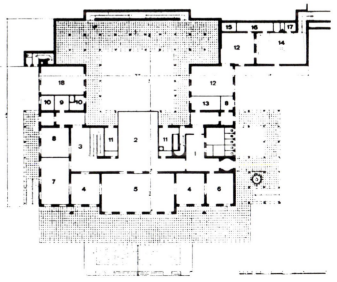

interior surfaces, an apt stylization of the classical repertory has been employed. For ornamental purposes, this stylization is adapted to compositions with Art Deco elements.

The most Modern work of Holzmeister in Ankara is the Presidential Palace (Figs. 59, 60). Modern expression is achieved in this building through the modification and stylization of classical elements, schemes and design principles. In this respect, the building reveals the particular character of Holzmeister's architecture. The plan of the palace is essentially symmetrical, or as Benevolo puts it, "instinctively symmetrical." Large halls are located on axes of symmetry; stairs are in the opposite direction but symmetrically disposed. Yet the wide porch with cantilevered eaves conceals the symmetry of the elevation. Inside, on axis, there is an atrium with a square pool in the center. The portico surrounding the atrium is composed of reductionist and simplified architectural elements. Ornamentation has been avoided except for the natural characteristics and texture of the material used throughout the whole building. The service block attached on the west provides a fit with the topography and, to a certain extent, upsets the symmetry of the whole. The building, with its modest scale and its relationship to setting, gave the impression of a large modern villa. "Above the downward sway of its stairs and the garden terraces ... the view of the wide-fronted building standing is simple, noble, dignified and impressive."[34]

Ernst Egli (1893-) worked in Turkey during 1927-1940 and 1953-1955 as an educator, consultant and architect. His major works are: the Conservatory of Music (1927-1928), the Court of Financial Appeals

Fig. 61 Egli, Court of Financial Appeals (Sayıştay), Ankara, 1928-1930.

(Sayıştay) (Fig. 61), the School of Commerce (1928-1930), the Ismet Paşa Institute for Girls (Fig. 62), the School of Political Science (1935-1936), and the Devres Villa in Istanbul (1932). Egli's architecture differs radically from Holzmeister's. For Egli, form and design principles such as neo-classical plan schemes, symmetry and axiality were not determining concepts. Even in the Conservatory, the interior courtyard, in terms of its scale and portico, is very different from Holzmeister's large-scale spaces. It resembles Ottoman courtyards more closely. His other works are modern not only in terms of plan but also in design principles and forms. For instance, the School of Commerce has a freer layout with respect to the size and location of its masses, and its elevation is similarly governed by the volumes behind it. The Ismet Paşa Institute for Girls exhibits characteristics such as *edelputz*, plastered flat walls, a horizontal mass finished with a narrow cornice, storeys described by long horizontal bands, and continuous window-sill lines.

The works of Egli, particularly the schools he built as the consultant architect to the Ministry of National Education, are also significant for their economy. This is an economy achieved not only through inexpensive building materials but through plans avoiding waste. In our opinion, as an educator and architect, Egli might be said to represent best the spirit of the young Republic.

Egli, who was assigned the reorganization of the curriculum of the Architecture Department of the Academy of Fine Arts, and who organized architectural education after central European models, was particularly influential in architectural circles of the initial years. Unlike the loud

Fig. 62 Egli, Ismetpaşa Institute for Girls, Ankara, 1930.

83

presence of a Holzmeister building, those of Egli are modest; yet their influence was more widespread and lasting. Egli was not a dogmatic modernist, but carried out his teaching (or his opportunity to mold architectural attitudes) with common sense and responsibility. While being a functionalist and anti-stylist, he never advocated crude borrowing. He advised and personally undertook careful consideration of local conditions and of Turkish architectural traditions.[35]

Among the factors that have been influential in the introduction and diffusion of modern architecture in Turkey were foreign-educated architects and the beginning of professional publications. The first architectural periodical, *Mimar*, appeared in 1931. Its name changed to *Arkitekt* in 1933, under the editorship of Zeki Selâh [Sayar], and it became a significant document of the architectural development of Turkey. Its fifty-year span to the 1970s documented and reviewed major projects and architectural writings. As such, the magazine has been a major source for our research since the civic buildings of the 1930s have been destroyed by the urbanization wave of the 1960s.

In 1932, Ziya enthusiastically advocated the "new art."[36] Burhan Arif, a city planner, in his article entitled "The Building of New Cities," advocated economical mass-housing to counteract land speculation, and gave *siedlung* examples, praising Ernst May.[37] In 1937, upon the request of the Ministry of State Monopolies, Taut assigned to the graduating students of the Academy a *siedlung* study.[38] This row-housing project, arranged in conformity with the prevailing laws and the Jansen master plan, provides a realistic approach to the most serious problem of the time. Articles protesting the commissioning of foreign architects and stating that there was a sufficient number of proficient Turkish architects began to appear in the 1930s.[39]

A second significant publication was Celâl Esat [Arseven]'s book, *Yeni Mimari*, 1931. As the first book in Turkey dealing with modern architecture, it introduced the general outlines of the establishment of CIAM, and the principles of the Modern Movement, the German Functionalists and Le Corbusier. To these can be added various articles, reports and books by Egli, Wagner, Reuter and Taut, published in newspapers, magazines and government reports.

The early period of Modern Turkish Architecture, extending from 1927 to World War II, can be viewed in three phases with distinct characteristics. First came the encounter with modern thinking and works. The phase of preparation and experimentation lasted approximately until about 1933. Then, under the impetus of the building program in Ankara, influenced by the works and origins of foreign architects and by the atmosphere of radical thought, a period of action was inaugurated. Young Turkish architects, whose commissions were limited to residences and small commercial buildings, took up the Modern Movement with gusto and considerable aptitude. Their works were essentially akin to those of the Vienna purists and to the early cubism of Le Corbusier.

The earliest known Modern building by a Turkish architect is the Bekır Bey House in Istanbul, designed by Sırrı Arif in 1929.[40] Sedat Hakkı [Eldem], A. Ziya [Kozanoğlu], Zeki Selâh [Sayar], Abidin [Mortaş], Hüsnü, Semih Rüstem, and Arif Hikmet were among the most popular.

Fig. 63 Holtay, Observatory of the University of Istanbul, Istanbul, 1934-1936.

Fig. 64 Zühtü, Mehmet Efendi Coffee Trade, Eminönü, Istanbul, 1932. Exterior.

Fig. 65 Zühtü, Mehmet Efendi Coffee Trade, Eminönü, Istanbul, 1932. Stairwell detail.

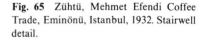

Among the buildings of the first phase, certain characteristics are recognizable. Plans are freely arranged, without rigid geometry (square or rectangular), but according to the nature and function of the constituent volumes, although still in geometrical forms. In a few purist examples, and particularly in houses, pre-determined geometrical frameworks are also used. In attached row-houses, the shape of the lot is, undoubtedly, a determinant. The house plan composed of unspecialized spaces is replaced in 1931-1933 by house plans composed of specialized spaces, shaped and sized according to their functions. In detached houses or apartment buildings, the plan is arranged around a large central hall which is not simply a circulation space. Service spaces are grouped together. In apartment buildings, this grouping has strained the functional relationship of the services with other volumes.[41] Spaces with circular plans are very popular. In residences, they are used mostly for dining and living spaces, terraces, and sometimes stairwells. Horizontal band windows and corner windows begin to gain wide acceptance. The overhanging eave is further shortened. Reinforced concrete structure or concrete slab construction and *edelputz* plaster is used.

In terms of approach, the examples in Ankara exhibit a more homogeneous appearance, while in Istanbul a diverse repertory is still apparent (Fig. 63). For instance, the semi-hexagonal projections, rightly compared by Aslanoğlu to the stairwells, halls and bay windows of the Chicago School,[42] are used in single houses and apartment buildings. In Istanbul all these forms are enriched by Art Deco elements. Among the Art Deco examples of these are Mehmet Efendi Coffee Trade (Figs. 64,65) in Eminönü, by Zühtü, 1932; Nazire Hanım residence in Maçka by Sırrı Arif; and the Bosfor Apartment House in Gümüşsuyu, by Macaroğlu and Livas Bey, 1932.

Barely five years after the construction of the Ministry of Health (Fig. 54), the Modern Movement had caught on particularly in graphics, calligraphy and interior design as well. The decorator Vedat Ömer produced abstract paintings and a Corbusian interior with Bauhaus furnishing for the movie *Istanbul Streets.*

The second phase (1933-1938) can be said to begin with Seyfettin Arkan's winning of the competition for one of the presidential pavilions, now the residence of the Minister of Foreign Affairs (Hariciye Köşkü) (Fig. 66). Time had come for Turkish architects to come into their own. Many public buildings of different scales were now designed by Turkish architects, through competitions or direct commissions. In this period the designs of the first women architects also started to appear in *Arkitekt*: Münevver Belen and Leman Tomsu, also a professor. They are principally known as the architects of People's Houses. Among the other leading architects of the period were Zeki Sayar, Bekir Ihsan, Rebii Gorbon, Rüknettin Güney, and Asım Kömürcüoğlu.

The characteristic designs and forms of this period exhibit certain consistencies. This is partly explained by the restrictions imposed by the Municipal Public Works Act (1933) and the dimensions prescribed by regulations, leading to a standard peculiar to Turkey. The architectural features of the period can be listed as follows:

In houses and public buildings, functionalist planning has been applied. Since layout was oriented by functional relationships, diverse programs and typological elements in public buildings did not allow for the emergence of certain schemes, while in apartment buildings special schemes were adopted. The hall as the central space of the house, explained by some researchers as a response to heating requirements, is an invariant element of this period. Schemes using a corridor instead of the central hall are fewer in number. In both houses and public buildings, there is an

Fig. 66 Arkan, Residence of the Minister of Foreign Affairs (Hariciye Köşkü), Ankara, 1933-1934.

acknowledged repertory of forms, rounded corners coupled with prismatic masses, horizontal strips separating the storeys, continuous, uninterrupted windowsill lines, window groups turning the corners. Circular plan spaces and their massing are less frequent compared to the preceding period (Fig. 67). Instead, rectangular plans with rounded corners are popular, particularly in entrances, balconies, terraces and stair halls. Flat or concealed roofs are widespread in spite of practical problems. In houses, balconies or wide continuous porches along the whole elevation are popular elements.[43] Toward the end of the period there is a change in scale and proportions, and a shift towards symmetrical arrangements is evident.

The competition for the Grand National Assembly may be taken as a convenient beginning for the third period. The entries and winning projects may be viewed as the indicators. After this date, projects, particularly those for public buildings, begin to show a Holzmeisterian tone. Actually, no substantial change occurred in planning and most of the architectural elements. Yet towards the end, particularly in public buildings, there was an increased tendency for symmetrical arrangements. To give a vertical effect on the facade, porticos composed of thin, two- or three-storey-high columns were used. Overhanging eaves began to appear again in the repertory and along with *edelputz* plaster, natural or artificial stone finishing was employed.

In apartment buildings, the norms prescribed by the Municipal Public Works Act produced an anonymous and standard look and were the determinants of cityscapes for years to come. Active in this period were Taut, Holzmeister, Bekir I. Ünal, A. Sabri Oran, K. Ahmet Aru, and Emin Onat, in addition to the architects of the preceding period.

Fig. 67 Taut, Faculty of Letters (Dil ve Tarih-Coğrafya Fakültesi), University of Ankara, 1937.

Modernism was predominant in the decade 1930-1940, but it paved the way for its own antithesis which can be defined through two developments. One is the protest against commissions given to foreign architects in Turkey. The other is the National Architecture Seminar initiated in the Academy of Fine Arts.

As early as 1933, articles were published in *Mimar* protesting the commissioning of foreign architects and gradually the protest turned into a campaign. The campaign actually addressed the public authorities who had control over investments. This protest was by no means unjustified. For instance, although Martin Elsaesser had agreed to work in collaboration with a Turkish architect on the Sümerbank Building and on the Ankara Cemetery, he refused to honor this agreement and was chastised by the Society of Turkish Architects. Another example was the dispute connected with the architectural competition for the Grand National Assembly. While competitors were invited from abroad, Turkish architects were excluded. Only after a vociferous campaign were Turkish architects given the chance to compete.

The protest, which originated from the sharing of a professional market, gradually acquired an ideological content. It became an opposition to the Modern spirit which was being identified with foreign architects and was therefore declared to be alien. In this reversal, the anti-Modernist thinking of National Socialists played a part. The German and Italian architecture exhibitions created a powerful echo in the single-party atmosphere of Turkey. Even in *Arkitekt*, itself a progressive and Republican publication, the rise of nationalism can be discerned. For instance, in 1938, the complete text of the letter against cubism and internationalism written by the president of AIA to President Roosevelt was published.[44]

This general account of the architecture of the decade will be concluded with two architects representative of different and parallel tendencies, Seyfettin Nasih Arkan and Sedat Hakkı Eldem.

Seyfettin Nasih Arkan (1902-1966), after graduating from the atelier of Vedat Tek, went to Germany on a scholarship and worked for Poelzig for five years. Earning Atatürk's praise for his design of the Residence of the Minister of Foreign Affairs (Hariciye Köşkü) (Fig. 66), he was asked to design the presidential summer residence in Florya (Fig. 68). In addition, his works included the Turkish Embassy in Tehran (1937), various branches of the Türk Ticaret Bankası and the Ottoman Bank (between 1949 and 1955), Sümerbank Pavilions in the Izmir International Fair (1937, 1944), worker housing in Kozlu and Üzülmez in Zonguldak (1934-1936), the Istanbul Power Station Complex (1943-1947), various residences and apartment buildings, sports and vacation facilities, and master plans.

Among the first works of Arkan, Dr. Ihsan Sami House in Suadiye (1933) is a Corbusier adaptation on pilotis. Çankaya and Florya are careful works unpretentious in appearance, exhibiting Bauhaus influences, fragmented plans with different functions juxtaposed, flat surfaces and large areas of glass. The horizontal, covered terrace of the Çankaya Prime Minister's residence, with its minimal columns and roof, is a reference to the atrium arrangement of Holzmeister in the Presidential Residence. The Üçler Apartments (Fig. 69) in Ayazpaşa also display a high quality of craftsmanship and a richness of design solutions as early as 1935. Arkan's

Fig. 68 Arkan, Presidential Summer Residence, Florya, Istanbul, 1934. Detail of interior. (Photo: Reha Günay)

Fig. 69 Arkan, Üçler Apartments, Ayazpaşa, Istanbul, 1935.

most famous work was the Municipalities Bank (Fig. 70) commissioned in 1935, through a competition. Its four-storey horizontal mass consists of two office wings joined in an L-form and rests on a podium-like ground floor. Its most interesting arrangements are inside, in the bank hall and director's storey, where the interior surfaces are shaped in an undulating manner. Along with the simple use of expensive material, the expressionist formation of the interior was an uncommon practice at the time.

Arkan's inclination toward expressionism can be noticed in the circular-plan of the Ankara Cinema, particularly in its massing and architectural elements. Workers' housing is another significant contribution. The *siedlungs* for the Zonguldak houses are designed with the flat roofs, small spans, and minimum areas of early functionalism. The Salih Bozok Villa in Suadiye (1939) diverges from his earlier style. This work at first can be seen as an interesting reference to the Second National Architectural Movement, with its high twin columns, its eaves and the symmetry of its sea elevation. Yet with the same elements, the double eaves of the roof and the symmetrical porch extending to the sea, it can also be regarded as an expressionist work.

Although Eldem has been totally identified with the National Architecture Seminar and thus is known as a leading theoretician, in this period it was his practice which best displayed the fruits of his research on architectural form. After his graduation from the Academy (1928) and his early Turkish house studies in Paris and Berlin (1929-1930), his search for a national architectural idiom was evident in 1932 in the projects he built in Maçka, Şişli and Heybeliada. Eldem developed an architectural attitude derived from his studies of the nineteenth-century Turkish house. He believed in the necessity of reinterpreting elements to arrive at a new synthesis in order to maintain historical continuity. In many of his works, particularly in houses, he insistently searched for possibilities and forms of this continuity. The central *sofa* element is a *leitmotif* which he

89

Fig. 70 Arkan, Municipalities Bank (Belediyeler Bankası, now İller Bankası), Ankara, 1937.

passionately tried to revive. It can appear as an oval hall in the J. Hanım House (Maçka/Istanbul, 1932)[45] and in the Ağaoğlu Residence (Maçka/Istanbul, 1938)[46], as an octagon, or with eyvans (a cross-plan with eyvans opening in four directions or T-plan opening in three). This search is most typically evident in the Ağaoğlu Residençe, coupled with a purist massing (Fig. 71). Though rather naive, it was one of the most interesting syntheses of form achieved by Eldem, but has since been demolished. A second *leitmotif* is the subdivision and window proportions of facade treatment. The window pattern on houses and on all his buildings has become a signature (Fig. 72).

Eldem's insistence upon the reinterpretation of traditional elements gives way to modern functionalism in competition projects or public buildings. In this respect, his most surprising work is the SATIE Building designed for the Electric Company. This building, constructed in 1934 and no longer extant today, had a Corbusian elevation with horizontal bank windows above free columns in front of a receding ground floor and an entrance with rounded corners and cubist massing.[47]

The competition design he prepared for the Istanbul Conservatory is also functionalist.[48] The Termal Hotel in Yalova, which he had secured through a competition, is totally modern and internationalist.[49] However, here as well, Eldem has divided the ground floor elevation into two storeys, arranging the windows of the upper part with diagonal braces and colored glass, connecting it to the traditional upper-window element. The General Directorate of State Monopolies which Eldem built in 1937 is a work that follows the Holzmeisterian line.[50]

It is difficult to answer the question, "With what kind of an expression can architecture externalize a search which has not been completely defined?" What is known and important is that there was an expectation of a new expression. The architectural and teaching activity of Egli,

Fig. 71 Eldem, Ağaoğlu Residence, Maçka, Istanbul, 1938.

Fig. 72 Eldem, Turkish Pavilion, New York World's Fair, 1939.

Holzmeister and others served as a catalyst. Turkish architects and Turkish architectural education owes a great deal to these masters. Yet it is the activity of a handful of Turkish architects, through their works, publications and organizations, which created a lively modern architectural atmosphere. If there had been a heroic side, in Corbusier's definition of the word, in the attempts to create an architecture of the Republic at a time when reformist ideology was most powerful, this aspect should not be sought in architectural activity alone. In fact, architecture was only a part of the total effort of these reform years.

NOTES

1. The major sources for the study of this period are *A Speech Delivered by Ghazi Mustapha Kemal, President of the Turkish Republic, October 1927* (Leipzig, 1929); D. Avcıoğlu, *Türkiye'nin Düzeni* (The Order of Turkey) (Ankara, 1960); S. Kili, *Türk Devrim Tarihi* (History of Turkish Revolution) (Istanbul, 1980); E. Kongar, *Türkiye'nin Toplumsal Yapısı* (Social Structure of Turkey) (Istanbul, 1976); K. Steinhaus, *Atatürk Devrimi Sosyolojisi* (*Sociologie der Türkischen Revolution*), M. Akkaş, tr. (Istanbul, 1973); S. Yerasimos, *Azgelişmişlik Sürecinde Türkiye* (Turkey: A Case Study in Underdevelopment), B. Kuzucu, tr. (Istanbul, 1973).

2. Cf. Avcıoğlu, *Türkiye'nin Düzeni*, p. 178; Steinhaus, *Atatürk Devrimi*, pp. 138-149.

3. I. Tekeli and I. Ortaylı, *Türkiye'de Belediyeciliğin Evrimi* (Development of the Municipal Order in Turkey) (Ankara, 1978), p. 47.

4. *Ibid.*, p. 45.

5. *Ibid.*, p. 88 and Table 1.

6. *Ibid.*, p. 91.

7. *Ibid.*

8. *Ibid.*, p. 92.

9. O. Şenyapılı, "Ankara 70" *Mimarlık* 3 (1970), p. 26 and n. 6.

10. F.R. Atay, *Çankaya* (Istanbul, 1980), p. 355.

11. N. von Bischoff, *Ankara: Türkiye'deki Yeni Oluşun Bir Izahı* (Ankara: An Interpretation of a New Beginning in Turkey, (Ankara, 1936), pp. 229-232.

12. S.I. Aralov, *Bir Sovyet Diplomatının Türkiye Hâtıraları* (Turkish Memoirs of a Soviet Diplomat), H.A. Ediz, tr. (Istanbul, 1967), p. 73.

13. Şenyapılı, "Ankara 70," p. 70.

14. von Bischoff, *Ankara*, p. 232.

15. Tekeli and Ortaylı, *Belediyecilik*, p. 44.

16. Atay, *Çankaya*, pp. 427-428.

17. T. Tayanç, *Sanayileşme Sürecinde 50 Yıl* (Fifty Years of Industrialization) (Istanbul, 1973), pp. 98-104.

18. Among the periodicals which should be consulted are *Hakimiyet-i Milliye*, *La Turquie Kemaliste* and *Nafia Işleri Dergisi*.

19. Tekeli and Ortaylı, *Belediyecilik*, p. 48.

20. Ü. Nalbantoğlu, *An Architectural and Historical Survey on the Development of the "Apartment Building" in Ankara: 1923-1950* (Ankara, 1981); I. Tekeli, "Türkiye Kentlerinde Apartmanlaşma Sürecinde Iki Aşama" (Two Stages in the "Apartmentalization Process" in Turkey) *Çevre* (Environment) 4 (1979), p. 79.

21. Quoted in Y. Yavuz, "Cumhuriyet Dönemi Ankara'sında Mimari Biçim Endişesi" (Concern with Architectural Form in Republican Ankara) *Mimarlık* 11-12 (November-December, 1973), p. 29.

22. For example, it is known that Atatürk himself chose Jansen's plan for Ankara and Holzmeister's design for the Grand National Assembly: *Arkitekt* 1 (January, 1938), p. 29 and I. Aslanoğlu, *Erken Cumhuriyet Dönemi Mimarlığı* (Early Republican Architecture), Ph.D. diss., M.E.T.U., Ankara, 1980, p. 75.

23. Tekeli and Ortaylı, *Belediyecilik*, pp. 40-41.

24. Nalbantoğlu, *Architectural and Historical Survey*, A:11, Appendix F; Ü. Alsaç, *Türkiye'deki Mimarlık Düşüncesinin Cumhuriyet Dönemindeki Evrimi* (Development of Architectural Thought in Turkey during the Republican Period) (Trabzon, 1976), pp. 215-227, contains a full list of foreign architects who practiced in Turkey.

25. D. Kuban, "Architecture and Ideology: The Atatürk Years," unpublished paper.

26. Tekeli and Ortaylı, *Belediyecilik*, p. 39.

27. *Hakimiyet-i Milliye*, January 3, 1927: quoted in Yavuz, "Cumhuriyet Dönemi," p. 28.

28. Nalbantoğlu, *Architectural and Historical Survey*, p. T-27.

29. Y.K. Karaosmanoğlu, *Ankara* (Istanbul, 1981), pp. 121-125.

30. *Elli Yıllık Yaşantımız* (Fifty Years of Turkish Life), Vol. I (Istanbul, 1973), p. 186.

31. L. Benevolo, *Histoire de l'architecture moderne* (Paris, 1979), Vol. II, p. 86; C. Jencks, *Mouvements modernes en architecture* (Bruxelles, 1977), pp. 53-54.

32. Aslanoğlu, *Erken Cumuriyet Dönemi*, p. 75.

33. The most complete presentation of Holzmeister's work is found in C. Holzmeister, *Clemens Holzmeister* (Vienna, 1982).

34. von Bischoff, *Ankara*, p. 137.

35. E. Egli, *Sinan, der Baumeister Osmanischer Glanzeit* (Stuttgart, 1954) is, for example, a careful and still current reference book on the great Turkish architect.

36. A. Ziya, "Yeni Sanat" (New Art) *Mimar* 4 (April, 1932), pp. 97-98.

37. B. Arif, "Yeni Şehirlerin İnkişafı ve 'Siedlung'lar' " (Development of New Cities and *Siedlungs*) *Mimar* 6 (June, 1932), pp. 213-216.

38. "Prof. Bruno Taut'un G.S.A. Son Sınıf Öğrencilerine Hazırlattığı İnhisarlar İdaresi Memurları İçin Tip ve Sıra Evler" (Type and Row-houses for State Monopolies Personnel) *Arkitekt* 8 (August, 1937), pp. 211-214.

39. Abidin [Mortaş], "Memlekette Türk Mimarının Yarınki Vaziyeti" (Turkish Architects' Future) *Arkitekt* 5 (May, 1933), pp. 129-130.

40. S. Arif, "Bekir Bey'in Evi" *Mimar* 1 (January, 1931), pp. 5-7; Aslanoğlu, *Erken Cumhuriyet Dönemi*, pp. 144-145.

41. Nalbantoğlu, *Architectural and Historical Survey*, p. T-90.

42. I. Aslanoğlu, "1930'lar Türk Mimarlığında Batı Etkileri" (Western Influences on the Turkish Architecture of the 1930s) in *Bedrettin Cömert'e Armağan* (Ankara, 1980), p. 551.

43. In the ten residences published by *Arkitekt* in 1937, the following characteristics are observed:

horizontal window strips	4 instances
roof terrace	8 instances
corner windows	9 instances
central hall	7 instances
corridor circulation	3 instances
continuous window sills	9 instances
continuous facade balcony	6 instances

44. *Arkitekt* 4 (April, 1938), p. 95.

45. Sedat Hakkı [Eldem], "J. Hanım Evi/Maçka," *Mimar* 6 (June, 1932), pp. 168-170.

46. See *Arkitekt* 9 (September, 1938), pp. 277-280.

47. Sedat Hakkı [Eldem], "Elektrik Şirketi Deposu/Fındıklı," *Mimar* 6 (June, 1934), pp. 159-162.

48. S.H. Eldem, "Müzik Öğretmen Okul Binası," *Arkitekt* 4 (April, 1938), pp. 10-13.

49. S.H. Eldem, "Yalova Termal Oteli," *Arkitekt* 3 (March, 1938), pp. 67-81.

50. S.H. Eldem, "İnhisarlar Umum Müdürlük Binası" *Arkitekt* 12 (December, 1937), pp. 315-324.

CHAPTER V

THE SECOND PERIOD OF NATIONAL ARCHITECTURE

Üstün Alsaç

For the first fifteen years of the Republic, Atatürk's opinions and actions had the weight of law. Thus, it is particularly important to note his attitudes towards the arts if we are to understand his impact on architecture. He does not seem to have been the supporter of extreme nationalism in the arts. He apparently felt that the Republic should develop its own art forms. Such an attitude is most clearly revealed in his ideas about music. Although he was personally fond of Turkish music, he supported the introduction of Western polyphonic forms. In fact, he used the radio extensively to disseminate the appreciation of Western music in Turkey. As for architecture, he does not seem to have favored the First National Movement. Its highly charged imagery and its symbolic references to a particular kind of Ottomanism were, in the end, not acceptable to him. One could even say that he must have sensed that many of his Westernizing reforms could be subverted under the guise of "nationalism." It is no accident, then, that the First National Movement was replaced at the end of the twenties by international functionalism.

The resurgence and rearticulation of regionalism and nationalism in architecture, though tentatively begun in the middle thirties, did not reach its full momentum until 1940, two years after Atatürk's death. The beginning of World War II was crucial in influencing the development of the Second National Movement. The economic crisis brought about by the war halted most construction programs. The import of building materials, such as steel, glass and cement, essential for modern construction, came to an abrupt end. Building regulations were revised in response to these shortages. Even those architects who had been protagonists of the Modern Movement were forced to turn to regional building materials and regional methods of construction. These building materials and methods of construction, however, had already been appropriated by the Second National Movement.

The psychological effect of the war also must not be underestimated. Though neutral, Turkey was totally surrounded by hostilities. Nationalism was called upon to create internal cohesion and to withstand external pressures. Whatever buildings were constructed during the war years reflect this atmosphere. That the florescence of the Second National Movement was intimately tied to the pressures of war is perhaps best demonstrated by the fact that the style, and its concomitant rhetoric, disappeared with the coming of peace. What appeared instead was a return to an internationalism which lasted out the decade and continued into the 1950s.

The death of Atatürk and the fact of war were only catalysts for the reappearance of regional tendencies in architecture. While not in official favor in the 1930s, they had not disappeared completely. They survived as ideas and as actual buildings. In addition, the architects responsible for developing them were still active during that decade. What is more, the younger generation of architects, though trained along the lines of functionalism and constructivism, began to take a stand on professional national exclusivity. Turkish architects argued that only they could truly represent the new spirit of the Republic in architecture. In addition, the new Ankara style, whether in its first constructivist version or its later monumentalist one, had not, it seems, been totally accepted by the people. Various comments, often derisive, circulated at the time about the cube-like nature of the "Modern" buildings.

Paving the way for a resurgence of regionalism was legislation passed in 1934 about the organization and responsibilities of the Ministry of Public Works. The text of the law is quite revealing: "The Ministry will see to it that a Turkish architectural style is developed in order to maintain a certain uniformity [in the environment]." Such a statement could be read as a desire for a national idiom. Finally, an event which assured the continued search for a regional identity was the founding by Sedat Hakkı Eldem of the "Seminar on National Architecture." With it began the

Fig. 73 Uçar, State Railroad Headquarters (T.C.D.D. Genel Müdürlüğü), Ankara, 1941.

Fig. 74 Onat and Eldem, Faculties of Sciences and Letters (Fen ve Edebiyat Fakülteleri), University of Istanbul, 1944.

Fig. 75 Utkular, Erginbaş and Güney, Istanbul Radio (Radyoevi), 1945.

systematic and sophisticated study of traditional architecture, a key influence in the formation of the new architectural generation. By 1940, Eldem published the principle theoretical statement on national idiom, "Yerli Mimariye Doğru" (Toward Local Architecture): *Arkitekt* 3-4 (1940). The Second National Movement had begun.

What was the definition of the national idiom? First of all, it was to be a product of the ground on which it stood. Climatic factors were important. Naturally, regional building materials and construction methods were to be used as well as native craftsmen. Historical building elements were to be modernized; earlier styles of Turkish architecture, civilian and rural building types, would be studied to serve as a source of inspiration. Modern building materials, useful because of their constructive properties, but unworthy because of their international character, could be used but had to be carefully covered. There was also a centralizing streak: the state was to adopt a specific style for all of its public buildings. A jury would be formed to determine this style and would control its application. Apart from this radical orientation, which was never fully realized, this architecture can be rightly called revivalism (Figs. 73, 74, 75).

When we look at similar movements elsewhere, we can see that such movements often display revivalist tendencies. They make use of architectural forms, constructions, building materials, styles, symbols of an earlier period or periods of a country which are considered as national, or at least as classical. They are viewed as being indigenous and therefore worthy of reusing. Such forms must be complex enough to be revived for modern use. Historical styles then serve as sources of inspiration, or at least they are used as standards of comparison for nationalism or classicism. Turkish architecture has rich architectural traditions for reference. While Anatolia had a long history of building before the arrival of the Turks, the Turks brought with them spatial concepts and forms from Central Asia and the Middle East. For nine hundred years these two traditions formed new syntheses, expressing themselves in various styles and producing unique building types. Both the First and the Second National Movements drew readily on this background (Fig. 76).

One can find similarities between the First and Second National Movements. First, they are both products of times of crises. There is a world war in the middle of each period. Both movements make use of historical forms. But similarities go only this far. Instead of the international eclecticism characteristic of the First National Movement, the second one has a more regional character. The latter makes use of rural or vernacular architecture. As far as historical styles are concerned, it restricts itself to that of the Anatolian Seljuks, whose symbols can only be understood within the national borders of Turkey.

Any revivalism can lead to controversial results; the Second National Movement is no exception. Nobody knew what kind of historical style

Fig. 76 Onat and Eldem, Faculty of Sciences (Fen Fakültesi), Ankara, 1945.

Fig. 77 Onat, a House in Kavaklıdere, Ankara, early 1940s. General view.

Fig. 78 Onat, a House in Kavaklıdere, Ankara, early 1940s. Detail of window.

could be defined as "national." Some earlier building types, which were part of the Anatolian heritage, were accepted as models by virtue of eminent domain. The desire to use elements of historical form or building materials resulted in an uneconomical use of modern construction or in irrational designs. Praise of hand-worked materials cannot be considered progressive in a world where everything is mechanized or industrialized. Earlier styles were products of their own time; they are born out of a necessity which may not exist any longer.

But revivalism also has positive aspects. After all, it seems to be a necessity to have at least one revivalist period before moving forward in modern architecture. It helps to deal with the overwhelming influence of the past. New constructions, building materials and functions need time to establish themselves before creating new forms and symbols. Until then there is a tendency to look back. Revivalism provides this opportunity. It is like searching the past for something lost, but it also reveals the irrationality of such a search. And when the repeating and revising has ended, minds are clear again to concentrate on the present or on the future. The process brings a better understanding for modern forms, constructions and functions. At least, this was the case in European and American architecture of the nineteenth and early twentieth centuries.

In his study, *Russische und Französische Revolutions-Architektur*, Adolf van Vogt states that shortly before and after revolutions, there is a tendency for rational, geometrical and dynamic structural forms. But after a revolution has established itself, there is a return, in about twenty years, to classical revivalism expressed in static forms. Van Vogt's ideas apply in a broad sense to Turkish architecture of the twentieth century. The rational-functionalistic architecture of the Republic appears between two revivalist (national) movements.

The regionalist concerns of the period led to extensive studies of regional and rural architectural forms. The rediscovery of the "Turkish House," which is no more a minor housing form than is the Japanese House, is the

Fig. 79 Eldem, Oriental Café (Şark Kahvesi), Taşlık, Istanbul, 1948-1950.

major contribution of the Second National Movement. Through this vehicle, Turkish architecture also has the potential of making a unique contribution to modern architecture (Figs. 77, 78, 79).

Nationalism in architecture found the support of an authority with an international reputation, Paul Bonatz (1870-1956). Bonatz first visited Turkey in 1942 as a member of the jury for the international competition of Atatürk's Mausoleum. His second visit about one year later was to accompany an exhibition on "The New German Architecture," traveling for propaganda purposes. Later that year he accepted the position of architectural consultant advisor-architect to the Turkish government. In 1946 he became professor of design at the Istanbul Technical University, and he held that position until 1955.

In his lectures and articles Bonatz criticized the Modern Movement (Figs. 80, 81). He claimed that every country was now searching for its cultural roots, and praised the use of "noble" building materials such as natural stone. The direct influence of German architecture may be difficult to pinpoint, but Bonatz reinforced nationalistic ideas. His activities were not restricted to teaching and writing alone; he was also a senior jury member in almost every competition where he supported the designs of his own students. He also designed some buildings in which he tried to put his ideas into practice. His predilection for the "Turkish House" expressed itself in a more formalistic than functionalistic manner within a residential quarter, Saraçoğlu Memur Evleri in Ankara.

The most important building of the period is Atatürk's Mausoleum (Anıtkabir) in Ankara. In 1941, an international competition was organized; in spite of the fact that the war was going on, there were forty-

Fig. 80 Balmumcu, National Exhibition Hall (Sergievi), Ankara, 1933-1934.

Fig. 81 Bonatz, Opera House (Büyük Tiyatro), Ankara, 1948. Conversion of the earlier National Exhibition Hall by Balmumcu.

six entries. Among the three designs presented to the Turkish government by the jury, there was one by two Turkish architects, Emin Onat and Orhan Arda, and this was ultimately built. The construction began in 1944 and the building opened in 1953 (Fig. 82).

The building is important in several respects. Its chief architect, Emin Onat (1908-1961), studied architecture in Switzerland under Otto Salvisberg, who was one of the leaders of functionalism in that country. In the jury were Paul Bonatz of Germany, Karoly Weichinger of Hungary and Ivar Tengbom of Norway, besides their Turkish colleagues. The building had to be redesigned several times before its completion in order to make it earthquake-proof or to reduce its construction costs. Its extended construction time saw changes in architectural concepts: it was begun when nationalistic ideas were at their peak and finished when a new internationalism was beginning to appear.

It is traditional as well as modern; it combines the Turkish tradition of *türbe* and the Anatolian tradition of mausoleum in a new, modern manner. It employs traditional building materials and construction methods as well as modern ones. It makes use of traditional decoration as well as of art

forms of non-Turkish origin such as reliefs and statues. It is monumental but still has a geometrical simplicity of fine proportions and excellent details. Its overall form does not revive the Seljuk-Ottoman commemorative architecture; it goes further back to older periods of Anatolian cultures, consciously claiming ownership of their architectural language.

As mentioned earlier in the chapter by Tekeli, this period witnessed significant developments in the architectural profession. The Engineering School in Istanbul became Istanbul Technical University in 1944, with a Faculty of Architecture. Its first dean was Emin Onat. Another was the First National Congress of Building in Ankara in 1948. It was the first forum where various problems of architecture, building and city planning were discussed. Both of these events are important; they are preliminary steps to a future which would begin to utilize scientific methods in solving architectural problems.

The ideas of a nationalism in architecture were discredited at the end of World War II. It was not only that the defeated ideology caused the waning of the Second National Movement, but that the reinforcement of national feelings was no longer necessary. Turkey opened itself to the world after a long and unwilling isolation: the end of the war activated commercial life.

The import of building materials began again. The country could put more of its resources into the building sector than it had been able to during the war. This caused an increase in the architectural commissions. An overall liberalism was beginning to appear. Architecturally it manifested itself in a new internationalism that would dominate the next decade. This new internationalism began with a rational functionalism, producing prismatic forms. The national competition for the Palace of Justice (Adliye Sarayı) in Istanbul marked this turning point: the winning design was not a revival of any kind; it was just a functional prism. Architects were Emin Onat and Sedat Hakkı Eldem; Paul Bonatz was on the jury; the year was 1949.

CHARACTERISTIC BUILDINGS AND THEIR ARCHITECTS

Ankara. Directorate of Turkish State Railways (Devlet Demir Yolları Genel Müdürlüğü). 1941. Bedri Uçar.

Istanbul. Faculties of Science and Letters of Istanbul University (Istanbul Üniversitesi Fen ve Edebiyat Fakülteleri). 1944. Emin Onat and Sedat Hakkı Eldem.

Ankara. Atatürk's Mausoleum (Anıtkabir). 1944-1953. Emin Onat and Orhan Arda.

Çanakkale. Monument of Victory and the Unknown Soldier (Çanakkale Zafer ve Meçhul Asker Anıtı). 1944. Feridun Kip, Ismail Utkular and Doğan Erginbaş.

Ankara. Faculty of Sciences (Fen Fakültesi). 1945. Emin Onat and Sedat Hakkı Eldem.

Ankara. Saraçoğlu Residential Quarter; now Namık Kemal Residential Quarter (Saraçoğlu Memur Evleri Mahallesi). 1945. Paul Bonatz.

Ankara. Opera House (Büyük Tiyatro). Rebuilt 1948. Paul Bonatz. First built as the Exhibition Hall in a constructivist style by Şevki Balmumcu, 1933-1934.

Istanbul. Şişli Mosque. 1945. Vasfi Egeli.

Istanbul. Radio House (Radyo Evi). 1945. Ismail Utkular, Doğan Erginbaş and Ömer Günay.

Istanbul. Amphitheater (Açıkhava Tiyatrosu). 1947. Nihat Yücel and Nahit Uysal.

Istanbul. Palace of Justice (Adliye Sarayı). 1949. Emin Onat and Sedat Hakkı Eldem.

Istanbul. Oriental Café (Taşlık Şark Kahvesi). 1948-1950. Sedat Hakkı Eldem.

Adana. Palace of Justice (Adliye Sarayı). 1945-1948. Abidin Mortaş, Nizamettin Doğu and Feyyaz Tüzüner.

Eskişehir. Railroad Station. Leylâ Baydar and Ferzan Baydar.

Istanbul. Inönü Stadium (Inönü Stadyomu). 1946. Şinasi Şahingiray, Fazıl Aysu and Violi Vietti.

Ankara. Grand Cinema (Büyük Sinema). 1949. Abidin Mortaş.

Istanbul. First Levent Residential Quarter (1. Levent Konut Sitesi). 1947. Kemal Ahmet Aru and Rebii Gorbon.

ARCHITECTURAL SCHOOLS

Güzel Sanatlar Akademisi (Academy of Fine Arts, founded in 1883 in Istanbul), Department of Architecture.

Istanbul Teknik Üniversitesi (Technical University of Istanbul, founded in 1773 as the Imperial School of Engineering, formed into a university in 1944), Faculty of Architecture.

Yıldız Teknik Okulu (Technical College, founded in 1911), Department of Architecture (since 1942).

PERIODICALS

Arkitekt (Architect, founded in 1931 as *Mimar*, named *Arkitekt* in 1935).

Yapı (Construction, 1941-1943).

Mimarlık (Architecture, 1944-1953).

Eser (Work, 1947-1948).

very imp

FOREIGN ARCHITECTS AND CITY PLANNERS IN TURKEY

Ernst Reuter, city planner, Germany
Henri Prost, city planner, France
Gustav Oelsner, city planner, Germany
Wilhelm Schutte, architect, Germany
Jean Walter, hospital designer, France
Violi Vietti, architect, Italy
F. Hillinger, architect, Germany
Paul Bonatz, architect, Germany
Le Corbusier, architect and city planner, France
Friedrich Hess, architect, Germany

EXHIBITIONS

Ankara. Yeni Alman Mimarisi (New German Architecture), 1943.

Ankara and Istanbul. Cumhuriyet Nafia Sergisi (Exhibition of the Ministry of Public Works), 1944.

Ankara and Istanbul. Ingiliz Mimarlık Sergisi (English Architecture), 1944.

Ankara, Istanbul, Izmir. Britanya Şehircilik Sergisi (City Planning in Britain), 1947.

Ankara. Iller Bankası Çalışmaları Sergisi (City Planning Activities of the Bank of Provinces), 1949.

OTHER EVENTS OF IMPORTANCE

Emin Onat is made honorary member of Royal Institute of British

Architects, 1946.

Turkish architects attend the first congress of U.I.A. in Lausanne, Switzerland, 1948. Turkish delegation consisting of: Emin Onat, Sedat Hakkı Eldem, Paul Bonatz, Kemali Söylemezoğlu, Harika Söylemezoğlu, and Apostol Pistikas.

SELECTED BIBLIOGRAPHY

Alsaç, Üstün. *Türkiye'deki Mimarlık Düşüncesinin Cumhuriyet Dönemindeki Evrimi* (Evolution of Architectural Thought in Turkey during the Republic). Ph.D. Diss., Trabzon, 1976.

Özer, Bülent. *Rejyonalizm, Üniversalizm ve Çağdaş Mimarimiz Üzerine Bir Deneme* (An Essay on Regionalism, Universalism and Our Contemporary Architecture). Istanbul, 1964, 2nd ed., 1970.

Sözen, Metin and Mete Tapan. *50 Yılın Türk Mimarisi* (Fifty Years of Turkish Architecture). Istanbul, 1973.

Anon. *Emin Onat*. Istanbul, 1962.

Van Vogt, Adolf. *Russische und Französische Revolutions-Architektur*. Cologne, 1974.

CHAPTER VI

INTERNATIONAL STYLE: LIBERALISM IN ARCHITECTURE

Mete Tapan

The built environment accurately reflects the economic, technological and social characteristics of a country. The differentiation of building types, changes in their characteristics according to new functional needs and the recurrence of certain types of buildings are indicators of the socio-economic system. Moreover, changes in any arena of the social realm influence the development of cities. Urban texture is affected by changes in the family structure, governmental system, economic policies and even by the international relations of a county. Thus, a scientific study of any built environment, whether it is planned or not, has to take into account sociological factors, and it is only through such an approach that a theoretical perspective on urbanization can be obtained.

The decade of the 1950s was a period of major transformation in many aspects of Turkish life. After a two-party system was established in 1946, the Democrat Party came to power with the elections on May 14, 1950. Development strategies were now to emphasize the role of the private sector. As mentioned by Ismail Cem, 1950 marked the revolution of the bourgeoisie.[1] However, the Turkish bourgeoisie differed widely from its Western counterpart. Unlike Europe, the rate of capital accumulation among the bourgeoisie in Turkey was considerably faster than the rate of development of production techniques:

> In Europe the production techniques kept up with the accumulation of capital within the private sector. Investment was thus channeled into industry. In Turkey this is not the case. Production means were insufficient and goods had to be imported at very high costs. Therefore, capital went into fast profit making, into commerce, into retailing, to the middleman and to other parasitic activities. In the 1960s, fifty percent of all capital investment went into the construction of luxury housing.[2]

This situation created conflicts in development strategies since the government was controlled by the interests of an underdeveloped bourgeoisie which nevertheless adopted Western models for its course of action.

During the 1950s Turkey depended on foreign credit for development. Investments were not made into heavy industry but into small inefficient industries. It was the merchants in urban areas and big landlords in rural areas who reaped the benefits without much risk. Most of the foreign credit was spent on agricultural machinery. In the beginning of the 1950s, the so-called "tractor years," big landowners gained control of agricultural production and small landowners, squeezed for cash, ended up selling their land. Thus began the massive migration to urban areas which also held the promise of jobs in the emerging industries. The urban growth rate, which had been three percent per annum since 1927, jumped to nine percent after 1950.[3]

This migration had a profound effect on the urban texture. Big cities such as Istanbul, Ankara and Izmir, where employment opportunities were high, became surrounded by gecekondus. These squatter areas, unsanitary and lacking infrastructure, came to house forty to fifty percent of the urban population.

This was also the period during which a lucrative real estate market developed and provided for the rapid growth of a semi-industrialized construction industry. The inflationary policies of the government led to massive investment in housing and land by individuals. Indeed, purchasing residential units or buying land was the most popular form of investment among the middle and the upper-middle classes.

Foreign aid, beginning with the Marshall Plan in 1947, Turkey's participation in the Korean War in 1951 and its admission to NATO in 1953, led to Turkey's fuller integration into the international economic system. Close alliance with the Western bloc reinforced liberal economic policies. The Law of Encouragement of Foreign Capital (Yabancı Sermayeyi Teşvik Kanunu) of 1947 was amended in 1951,[4] and was replaced by an even more liberal law on January 18, 1954.[5] The influx of foreign capital, however, in addition to foreign aid resulted in inflation and in greater foreign dependency.

This total reorientation of the economy naturally brought about the need for new building types and new modes of transportation. Whereas previously government investments were concentrated on building railroad networks, the government was now compelled to develop highways and urban arteries. Whereas previously owners of status buildings had to content themselves with local materials, now the available foreign exchange allowed them to import luxury finishes. Expensive residential units became as much a status symbol as they were real estate investment.

Close ties with the West brought about the use of new construction methods. International stylistic and formal concepts became more accessible. Because of this exposure, Turkish architects developed an eclectic approach. Eclecticism, as Bülent Özer has emphasized, is a meaningful phenomenon in building as long as it does not become systematized in the hands of architects. Borrowing from conclusions

Fig. 83 AHE Mimarlık, Aru, Emiroğlu, Erol, Handan, and Suher, Sheraton Hotel, Istanbul, 1958-1974.

reached elsewhere in architecture and being inspired by others is an inevitable consequence of our time. In this age of communication, it is impossible not to be influenced; but eclecticism can serve a positive purpose only if its premises are adapted properly to local conditions.[6]

Unfortunately, one cannot find such a positive approach in the buildings constructed in the decade 1950-1960. The architecture of this era exhibits inconsistencies within its own chronology in the approach to form. Facade treatments, which had been heavily influenced by Ottoman and especially Anatolian models during the Second National Movement of the previous decade, are now simple and rational and closely follow the ideas of the International Style. Plan and form solutions are prismatic in nature. Rectangles and squares, which are functional geometric elements, predominate in site plans. The grid system is used extensively on facades. A forerunner of this trend was the Istanbul Hilton Hotel, a joint venture of Skidmore, Owings and Merrill, and Sedat H. Eldem (Fig. 86).

Towards the end of the decade, inspired by Rolf Gutbrod's lectures at Istanbul Technical University (1957-1959), examples of organic architecture begin to appear. For example, the Istanbul Sheraton Hotel deviates from the prevailing principles of simple massing in reaction to the accepted forms of the 1950s (Fig. 83). Obviously, Gutbrod and Piccinato, who were on the jury, influenced the selection of this particular solution.

These stylistic problems aside, other major developments took place which would change the picture of architecture and the architectural profession. First, the rapid growth of cities made comprehensive master planning a necessity. Second, the construction industry expanded rapidly to answer increasing demand. Third, a law governing building was introduced in the Grand National Assembly in 1951. In an attempt to regulate and discipline architectural activity, the Ministry of Public Works issued new regulations for planning and architectural competitions.

107

Finally, the Turkish Chamber of Architects was established by the Law no. 6235 of 1954. This body was to act as a public service organization within the larger context of the Joint Chambers of Engineers and Architects.

Similar to the quick adaptation of Western economic and social models, contemporary architectural trends from other countries were also easily absorbed. Various architectural solutions published in journals were copied with no regard to appropriateness. Regional characteristics were ignored. Curtainwall construction came into use throughout the country. A facade treatment appropriate for Ankara was also proposed for humid or arid and hot parts of the country. The competition for the Municipality of Urfa is a case in point.

Obviously, this phenomenon was the result of Turkish architectural education. Architects, in an attempt to find solutions to new building types, turned to Western examples as their only source of information. Unfortunately, due to the lack of technical know-how, the Turkish examples lacked the quality of the Western models and most of them remained at the project stage. Those few that were completed not only cost a great deal more than anticipated but also underwent modifications during construction. As a result, mere imitations of Western architecture proved to be unsuccessful.

During this decade a new approach was adopted in architectural education. Architects such as Bruno Zevi, Rolf Gutbrod and Richard Neutra introduced students to current architectural movements. At first, students were tempted to imitate the International Style as can be seen from the treatment of forms in their projects. Later, the tenets of the International Style were further naturalized and internalized within the educational system because the faculty of the architectural schools had had the opportunity to study and practice in Europe and the United States. As a result of this adaptation, toward the end of the decade undergraduate and graduate theses in Istanbul Technical University began to take up new themes which dealt with basic issues in architecture such as the control of natural light, acoustics and the nature of building materials.

Fig. 84 Eldem and Onat, Palace of Justice (Adliye Sarayı), Istanbul, 1949.

In practice, the competition for the Istanbul Palace of Justice (Adliye Sarayı, 1948) marked the shift from the Second National Movement to the International Style. A rational approach was the order of the day. W.M. Dudok, a well-known rationalist, was on the jury. The competition was won by Sedat Hakkı Eldem and Emin Onat, two educators. A different attitude toward structure was now evident; the reinforced concrete structure was clearly expressed on the facade. However, in the treatment of the roof and the openings the influence of the Second National Movement was still discernable. The building consisted of a rectangular mass with three outrider blocks. This disposition of elements was intended to break the massive presence of the building in order to attain a harmonious scale with its neighboring historical buildings. Although one cannot say that it did so very successfully, the building was nevertheless important as a forerunner of the International Style (Fig. 84).

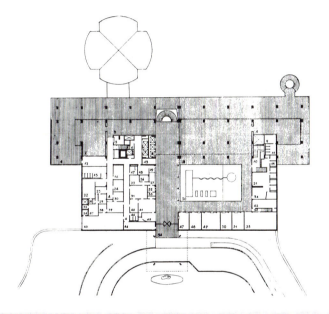

Fig. 85 Skidmore, Owings and Merrill, and Eldem, Hilton Hotel, Istanbul, 1952. Plan of lobby floor before extension. Interior courtyard of the shopping arcade and the vaulted structure of the nightclub pavilion incorporate elements of traditional architecture.

Fig. 86 Skidmore, Owings and Merrill, and Eldem, Hilton Hotel, Istanbul, 1952. View of the Bosporus elevation of the hotel after extension.

Fig. 87 Zıpçı, Akın and Ertan, Çınar Hotel, Istanbul, completed 1959.

The competitions for the Hilton Hotel (1952) and the Istanbul City Hall (Belediye Sarayı, 1953) set the predominant architectural trend for the decade. The Hilton Hotel is the most successful and influential example of the International Style, and the precursor of high-rise hotels in Turkey (Figs. 85, 86). Elements of traditional architecture were incorporated into the arcaded shopping complex and into the shell structure of the nightclub. The vast ground-floor lobby was taken out of its commercial hotel mold and oriented toward the Bosporus. The German construction firm which built this hotel introduced contemporary high-rise building technology to Turkey. The hotel became a model for many buildings. For example, the Çınar Hotel, built in 1959 by Rana Zıpçı, Ahmet Akın and Emin Ertan, displays the same disposition of masses on a smaller scale (Fig. 87). The Hilton Hotel itself, on its prominent site overlooking the Bosporus, has remained as an important presence in the silhouette of Istanbul, even with its later extension.

The winner of the competition for the Istanbul City Hall was Nevzat Erol (Fig. 88). All competition entries clearly showed the widening impact of the International Style. Many, including the winning one, had a common solution: a main block of offices in the form of a prism and a lower block of council rooms attached to it. This schematic arrangement was followed in many later projects. In the winning design the facade treatment included panels of small colored tiles; the overall percentage of window to wall, however, was greatly increased, a foreshadowing of later window-walls. All references to regional architecture had been eliminated. Characteristic for these types of buildings was the open plan of the ground floor space which was designated as a multi-purpose foyer.

Turkey's first skyscraper designed for commercial office space was the Emek Building (1959) by Enver Tokay and Ilhan Tayman (Fig. 89). It was also the first curtainwall building. The office tower was combined with a lower block of shops and public facilities. This functional disposition was repeated in later commercial buildings. The Emek Building was designed and executed solely by Turkish architects and engineers. Its success encouraged further ventures into reinforced concrete technology, and the

Fig. 88 Erol, City Hall (Belediye Sarayı), Istanbul, 1953. Its columnar base, its free-form roof structure, its grid facade and recessed windows introduce the International Style into the heart of the old city.

Fig. 89 Tokay and Tayman, Emek Building, Ankara, 1959-1964.

First skyscraper

need for high-rise buildings, hotels, apartments and office buildings with large column-free spaces led to the quick mastery of this technology.

A typical building designed at the end of the decade, the General Directorate of the State Waterworks, reflects the developed common architectural idiom in its form, structural system and varied floor plans. Designed by Behruz Çinici, Teoman Doruk and Enver Tokay and completed in 1964, this building has a rectangular tower of offices built on a podium and a separate lower auditorium block (Figs. 90, 91).

Fig. 90 Çinici, Doruk and Tokay, General Directorate of State Waterworks (Devlet Su Işleri), Ankara, completed 1964.

Fig. 91 Çinici, Doruk and Tokay, General Directorate of State Waterworks (Devlet Su Işleri), Ankara, completed 1964. Ground floor plan.

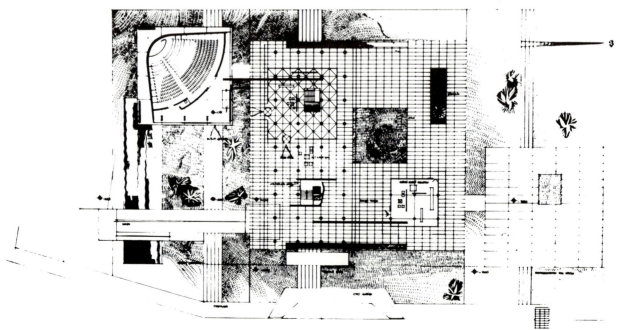

Among other important commercial and government buildings designed in the 1950s should be mentioned the Ulus Center (Ankara, 1954) by Orhan Bozkurt, Orhan Bolak and Gazanfer Beken with its lens-like office tower attached to banks of low-rise units (Figs. 92, 93); the Etibank Headquarters (Ankara, 1955-1960) by Tuğrul Devres and Vedat Özsan with its monumentalizing concave facades (Figs. 94, 95); and the Grand Hotel (Büyük Ankara, 1958-1965) by M. Sauger with its brutalist facade treatment and prismatic plan (Fig. 96). New technology was also used for new types of buildings such as the Karatepe Open Air Museum at Adana (Fig. 97, 98) by Turgut Cansever, with its poured concrete roof slabs; in the Anadolu Club in Büyükada, Istanbul, by Turgut Cansever and Abdurrahman Hancı, with its meticulously crafted window treatments and jewel-box finishes (Fig. 99); and in the complex of retail shops (Manifaturacılar Çarşısı) by Doğan Tekeli, Sami Sisa and Metin Hepgüler, with its low-rise buildings organized around courts (Fig. 100).

Fig. 92 Bozkurt, Bolak and Beken, Ulus Center, Ankara, 1954.

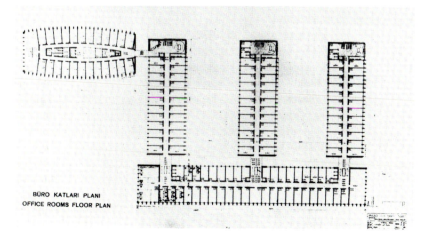

BÜRO KATLARI PLANI
OFFICE ROOMS FLOOR PLAN

Fig. 93 Bozkurt, Bolak and Beken, Ulus Center, Ankara, 1954. A typical office floor plan.

Fig. 94 Devres and Özsan, Etibank Headquarters, Ankara, 1955-1960.

Fig. 95 Devres and Özsan, Etibank Headquarters, Ankara, 1955-1960. Second-level plan.

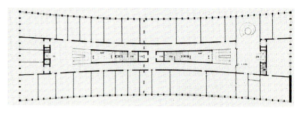

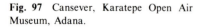

Fig. 96 Sauger, Grand Hotel (Büyük Ankara), Ankara, 1958-1965.

Fig. 97 Cansever, Karatepe Open Air Museum, Adana.

Fig. 98 Cansever, Karatepe Open Air Museum, Adana. Plan.

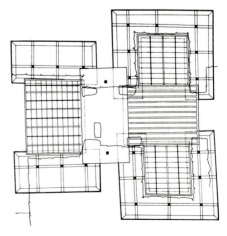

Fig. 99 Cansever and Hancı, Anadolu Club, Büyükada, Istanbul, 1959.

Fig. 100 Tekeli, Sisa and Hepgüler, Complex of Retail Shops (Manifaturacılar Çarşısı), Istanbul, 1959.

Fig. 101 Baysal and Birsel, Hukukçular Apartments, Istanbul, 1960-1961.

The stylistic and constructional changes manifested in commercial and public buildings were reflected to some degree in the housing sector. A prominent example of the new high-rise residential development for the middle and upper-middle classes is the Hukukçular Apartments (Istanbul, 1960-1961) by Haluk Baysal and Melih Birsel, with echoes of a Corbusian idiom (Fig. 101). Much more influential in shaping the cityscape were the Fourth Levent Development and the Ataköy Development. The contribution of these developments to housing in Turkey will be described in the last chapter. It should be noted, however, that the Levent Development was the first to combine single residences, row houses and multi-storey apartments for a mix of different income groups. The massing of the buildings and the shaping of the exterior space became a model for other projects. The Ataköy Development, mainly of multi-storey apartments, is an example of rapid construction with the use of reinforced concrete for high-rises and masonry for low-rise buildings (Fig. 102). As such, it became an easily replicable model in construction techniques. The booming construction triggered the production of new building materials: prefabricated panels, fixtures, plumbing supplies and finishes. But these new industries did not reach their full capacity until later decades.

Fig. 102 Menteşe and Project Office of the Emlâk Kredi Bankası, Ataköy Development, Istanbul, Phase I, 1961.

Urban life entered into a transitional period. The government made various attempts to extend planning nationwide, to establish a building policy and to regulate multiple ownership. New legislation required all municipalities with a population of 5000 or over to follow a master plan. With Law no. 7116 of 1958, the Ministry of Reconstruction and Settlement was established to coordinate and regulate all building activities. Yet these measures could not control the breakneck pace of urban expansion. With the shift in emphasis from railways to highways, major arteries came into being. Urban areas began to expand along intercity highways, and in fact, new urban areas along highways began to develop even in rural Turkey. The Istanbul-Izmir corridor of 100 kilometers, for example, has since become a metropolitan area.[7] In addition, the migration from rural areas into major urban centers led to the encirclement of old urban centers by rings of squatter housing. Such an influx created a crisis in municipal services, social and political problems, and finally, a questioning of the goals and ethics of the architectural profession itself.

Thus, the failure to implement controls and the absence of an infrastructure of sufficient capacity led to a disastrous expansion of the urban areas. It cannot be said that during the 1950s the relationship between resources and goals was examined properly and established with social welfare purposes in mind. This period, therefore, emerges as a decade of paradoxes with conflicting social needs, economic goals and technology. Future alternatives in architectural practice and thought should be considered in the light of this era.

NOTES

1. Ismail Cem, *Türkiye'de Geri Kalmışlığın Tarihi* (History of Underdevelopment in Turkey), 7th ed. (Istanbul, 1979), p. 334.

2. *Ibid.*, pp. 316-317.

3. *Ibid.*, p. 451.

4. The amendments of 1951 were favorable to countries providing capital. For example, a portion of annual profits not exceeding 10 percent of the capital invested in Turkey during the same year could be transferred out of the country. In addition, foreign investors were given the same rights and privileges as Turkish investors. Cf. Stefanos Yerasimos, *Azgelişmişlik Sürecinde Türkiye* (Turkey: A Case Study of Underdevelopment), 3rd ed. (Istanbul, 1980), p. 723.

5. This law was aimed at encouraging industrial development. Yet most of the new industries established consisted of component assembly plants and domestic industry was rendered heavily dependent on foreign imports.

6. Bülent Özer, *Rejyonalizm, Üniversalizm ve Çağdaş Mimarimiz Üzerine Bir Deneme* (An Essay on Regionalism, Universalism and Our Contemporary Architecture), 2nd ed. (Istanbul, 1964), p. 74.

7. Orhan Göçer, *Ülke Planlaması İçinde Gelişme Aksları, Şehirsel Gelişme Merkezleri Ilkeleri ve Türkiye İçin Bir Model Denemesi* (Axes of Development in Country Planning, Principles for the Development of Urban Centers and a Proposed Model for Turkey), (Istanbul, 1977), p. 223.

CHAPTER VII

PLURALISM TAKES COMMAND: THE TURKISH ARCHITECTURAL SCENE TODAY

Atilla Yücel

In an inquiry into the current thinking of the profession, published in 1970 by the Turkish Chamber of Architects, almost all responses were in essential agreement on two points: the growing interest of architects in social issues, and their search for a new formal vocabulary outside the prevailing canons of the International Style.[1] In fact, these two points have been continuously stressed as the most important issues confronting Turkish architects during the last two decades. This chapter will consider the rising interest in social problems together with the search for a new vocabulary, and will examine the degree to which the development of technological tools adopted in these processes has been successful. As the process covered by this analysis is still in progress, our conclusions may be incomplete and even self-contradictory. Yet, no predictions can be made about the future direction of these processes.

THE SOCIAL CONTEXT

The social change in Turkey has been discussed elsewhere in this book.[2] Therefore, we shall neither attempt to analyze the social history of the architecture of the last two decades nor argue that such a context would explain all the formal achievements of the architectural end product. However, it is strongly believed that there exists a causal relationship between social development and architectural ideologies and trends. But such a causality is indirect; it operates implicitly rather than in a predictable, deterministic fashion, and can only be discerned through the appearance of some new forms. Social forces act through a metalinguistic medium, that is, through current architectural ideologies.

To begin with, we shall attempt to describe the main outlines of the social milieu of the 1960s in which today's architectural thoughts as well as programs have been generated. Later, architectural activities, architectural theory as well as practice, will be reviewed in detail. These will provide a basis for evaluating more accurately the degree to which the milieu has influenced the production of form and also to what extent its beliefs and programs have been realized.

An important event which resulted in a series of new social, cultural, and economic departures was the military intervention of 1960. This coup not ony ended the oppressive rule of the Democrat Party but also led to reformist movements and new democratic institutions. The 1961 Constitution allowed broader freedom of expression and of association. New legislation increased the power and the influence of labor unions and professional organizations. Previously censored expressions of social thought and ideologies, and politically engaged literature and art now flourished in the freer atmosphere. The aspirations of the masses were given voice by the media, which in turn acted as a catalyst to their demands. In all, social and political issues were now actively taken up by all segments of Turkish society.

The new Constitution also established bureaucratic and economic mechanisms. After ten years of chaotic liberalism, a planned economy was again adopted. Consequently, economic, social and spatial planning concepts were introduced. The objectives were a rapid industrialization of the country and a more equitable distribution of income. This policy soon led to a growth rate of seven percent and a gradual development of large industrial complexes. But with the neglect of the agricultural sector, rural immigrants began to overwhelm the developing urban areas.

At the same time, closer and multilateral economic relations with the West gained momentum. These relations, with the OECD or the Council of Europe or the EEC, strengthened the pluralistic atmosphere created by the new Constitution and reinforced the process of democratization. In the resulting atmosphere, there was a proliferation of publications of a diversity unknown in Turkey until then. Social realism became a new tendency in plastic arts as well as in literature. The general trend was inevitably a new "opening to the left," and this left-wing movement influenced all intellectual and artistic activities and milieux, including those of architecture.

The closer relationship with the Western world affected not only intellectual life and institutions but also lifestyles. As a result of rapid urbanization a consumer society began to form. This trend was more widespread than in the 1950s, when it had been primarily limited to a privileged elite. At the same time, the newly developing industries produced consumer goods for the captive domestic market. Cars, TV sets, fashion goods, as well as expensive building materials, were becoming an inseparable part of the new urban way of life. Despite the developmental goals of the Five-Year Plans, this consumer prodigality was beyond the capacity of the national economy. Thus, major social problems created by the rapid industrialization and urbanization remained unsolved. These included urban growth, housing, environmental and ecological problems, as well as those created by the rapid cultural change and changing values.

Antagonistic forces resulting from the raised expectations of urbanized masses, the limited capacity of the emerging industries; the need for efficiency in governmental bodies within the framework of the democratic constitution, and the stance and influence of the intellectual elite created a dilemma. There was a continuous search for new models and solutions. In the mid- and late 1960s, incessant debates on democracy, socialism and nationalism took place in the mass media.[3] Influenced by the atmosphere of May 1968, this growing conflict came to a head in the early seventies, and subsequent democratic governments were faced with the oil crisis and with a growing anarchy of the late seventies. Their inability to deal with these problems culminated in the conclusive military intervention of 1980. Despite a great deal of social unrest, the two decades between 1960 and 1980 saw important new developments: the growth of industry and business, the emergence of a pluralistic world view and new concepts introduced by it, the establishment of an urban way of life with its concomitant attitudes and values, and the rise of social consciousness which pervaded current thought. These constitute the causal background for the architectural ideas of the last two decades.

PROBLEMS, CONCEPTS AND IDEOLOGIES

This socioeconomic background has manifested itself through functional, organizational or intellectual contexts. The latter are principally new building programs, changing architecture, activities of professional associations, and architectural theories, tendencies and ideologies either imported or generated by the professional intelligentsia.

New Programs, Needs and Constraints

Competitions, generally held by the Ministry of Public Works or other governmental offices, were an important arena for architectural activity of the period. Some of them, particularly in the 1960s, were organized for the social programs of the state. Hospitals, high schools and large university campuses were among the more significant architectural works of the period. The growing bureaucratic machine was also in need of new space for its expanding programs. Thus, competitions were organized for a series of town halls, government offices and ministries. However, the limitations of competition regulations obstructed innovative design ideas and generally produced insignificant results.

More important were the office building programs of the mid-1970s, promoted by big business and state enterprises. Very large programs for the latter, which called for new typological, structural and technical solutions, or prestige buildings for the former allowed a free interpretation of forms. Similar occasions for architectural creativity can be found in the tourist industry. Large hotels or holiday villages have produced some interesting examples. The most interesting opportunities for architectural experiments in housing have been provided either by resort villages (second houses) or by luxury primary residences. Both represent in program and form the most obvious examples of the consumer ideals of the ruling taste of the period.

The new functional programs of the expanding industry have produced the best examples of advanced industrialized building systems and techniques, demanding a completely new approach and know-how. The growing attention to the conservation and rehabilitation programs, more than a mere technical knowledge of restoration, required a growing cultural consciousness and sensitivity on the part of architects.

Architectural Education

These two decades also witnessed a series of reforms in the programs of existing schools of architecture, and the establishment of new ones. Among the old schools, the Istanbul Technical University was the first to review its curriculum and to look for new models. Already in the late 1950s, eminent foreign teachers such as Bruno Zevi or Rolf Gutbrod had taught or lectured at the Faculty of Architecture. The influence of the anti-International Style lectures soon manifested itself in the architectural works of the early 1960s.[4] At the same time, a more scientific approach to architecture was becoming popular among the younger faculty of the university. They were influenced by the empirical and positivistic architectural approaches developed in British and American universities. Finally, the need for a more socially conscious architecture was advocated by the same new generation.

The existing architectural schools broke away from their original models, German Technische Hochschule model (ITU) or French Beaux-Arts roots (Academy of Fine Arts). The most important of the new schools, the Middle East Technical University, was based on the American model. Onto the traditional roots of architectural education were grafted new orientations and these now yielded a richer, syncretic medium for future growth. New concepts such as scientific analytical studies and systematic design, objective methods for environmental control and architectural science, energy, environment and energy-conscious designs, and cybernetic or semiotic approaches to architecture were introduced into the curriculum of the major schools of architecture.[5] Between 1968 and 1979, these schools were also arenas of an active political debate. However, the relationship between sociopolitical utopia and the very essence of architecture could not be established in the endless discussions.

Social Conditions and Professional Associations

Although political discussions in the schools did not have an influence on architectural issues, the political stance of the professional organizations did. Since the 1950s, the Turkish Chamber of Architects had become more effective in protecting the professional rights of its members and more efficient in controlling the building activity. Parallel to its growing influence was an increase in the number of architects. In the late 1960s, the new schools and faculties of architecture were founded in Izmir, Istanbul, Ankara, Trabzon, Konya and Edirne.

But the increase in number of architects was also accompanied by a proletarianization of the profession.[6] In the 1960s, its economic status was still tolerable. The rapid development of large cities ensured employment for architects. The syndical activity of the Chamber of Architects was focused on widening and increasing the architects' share in the building market. By the mid-1970s, unemployment became an acute problem. Consequently, the architects came to constitute a radical opposition group supported by their own professional organization. Their rapid proletarianization was paralleled by recession, rising inflation, and a breakdown of investment programs causing major crisis in the building industry.[7]

This opposition culminated in leftist criticism which attributed the defects of the built environment to the extravagances of the economic order. The scope of this criticism established a solidarity with the working class and its political doctrines. This left-wing architectural criticism had two facets: first a Marxist—and very often a Marxian—-methodology and terminology; and at the same time, a nationalistic content. Thus, it remained nationalist—or patriotic—in defending the national professional rights, initiating campaigns, movements, or slogans such as "rely on our own forces" and "New National Architecture," or defending the national historical heritage, while using a Marxist terminology and a materialistic approach in its criticism.[8]

By the mid-1970s, this movement, led by the Chamber of Architects, had reached its climax and then gradually lost its thrust in the depoliticized atmosphere of the 1980s. But at the same time, it developed a greater theoretical content. Problems relating to form, meaning and design came to be reconsidered. Social criticism thus criticized itself, trying to establish theoretical relationships with other approaches such as structuralism or semiotics. It placed greater emphasis on history, aiming at a more synthetic architectural ideology and a theoretically grounded historical criticism.[9]

During the period of its preeminence, social criticism had concerned itself with form only in two cases. First, in an attempt to create the so-called "New National Architecture," it unavoidably referred to the two earlier National Movements, and provided them with a social content. Second, it searched for a new theoretical synthesis, inspired by the work of Tafuri and structuralism, and with the latter's impact on Marxist thought.

Turkey's openness to the Western world, coupled with the intensification of information flow, made the architectural milieu of the country vulnerable to the current trends of the other parts of the world. Cross-cultural influences generally manifested themselves in formal tendencies rather than in a coherent ideological unity. Thus, formal tendencies such as organic-Wrightian or *Organhaft* have been "carried" by the influential lectures of Zevi and Gutbrod or by their Turkish followers, and by architectural periodicals publishing the works of Niemeyer, Aalto, Bakema, Tange, and finally Kahn.[10]

These formal tendencies have been neither firmly advocated nor severely opposed by Turkish critics and polemicists. But they have been criticized as a total phenomenon precisely because they were an arbitrary choice. Among these critics, Bülent Özer described this general trend of borrowed forms from the standpoint of their relevance to the "actual data."[11] According to him, this attitude is an eclecticism,[12] and that in architecture different fashions cannot be adopted arbitrarily. He stresses the importance of a skeptical attitude and more conscious objective thought before "directly importing Western forms."[13] Özer's point of view is echoed by many others who condemn superficiality especially in architectural competitions.[14] Among them, Üstün Alsaç seems more favorable to new brutalism because the brutalist approach is more reconcilable with regional and national realities, what Özer calls "actual data."[15]

Some critics made use of the classical duality, that of rational and irrational forms or attitudes, in their categorization.[16] But it seems that these concepts remained vague and rather abstract. The fact that the same authors condemned *a priori* formal choices and at the same time adopted categoric classifications merely based on formal configurations remains a paradox.

But the term rationalism was also used to describe relevance to real conditions as in "rational attitude."[17] From this standpoint, rationalism, or rationality, merely advocates the best adaptation to environmental constraints and should thus be seen as a more scientific approach to design. Could not, then, be considered closer to regionalism? This seems very plausible when one reads Kortan, who criticizes some "articulated small-block" schemes which repeat, exactly like the functional prisms which they were meant to replace, the same layout principles on every site, no matter what the climatic, thus regional, conditions.[18] Regionalism could, moreover, be condemned as any other categorical concept and an "ism" like the others, and also because of its relationship with history.

Among the theoretical discussions of these two decades, the key issue has been history. Should it be implicit as it was in the case of regionalism, or explicit as in the current work of many architects, or in fields such as conservation where the subject matter implies an irrefutable historical element? Yet, it is also true that even if there had not been direct polemics on formal tendencies such as organic architecture, *Organhaft*, or new-brutalism, a debate on the interpretation of history would have already begun in the early 1960s around the so-called New Regionalism.

We consider that regionalism is a complete expression of an environment which is determined by economic, historical and cultural factors rather than by preconceived formal concepts. In Turkey, as in many other countries, the question of regionalism in architecture provides us with the opportunity to examine the relationship between buildings themselves and their cultural environment.[19] Having advocated such an Anatolian regionalism, Kuban later qualified it as the "real way of modern architecture," for it was also the very "interpretation of environmental conditions."[20] Özer condemned this view as being "imprecise, eclectic, romantic, utopian and self-contradictory." He also argued that Kuban, although using a different terminology and argumentation, was repeating the old-fashioned nationalist discourse of the National Movements.[21]

Later, the same term, regionalism, was used by others in a context more closely related to tradition and history. In an analysis of contemporary Turkish architecture, essentially through a retrospective review of his own work, Sedat Eldem exposed a unified version of regionalism as a synthesis of historical, regional, and economic-nationalist identities.[22] He can be seen as an exponent of the National Movement, the new regionalist concepts and even of the political criticism advocated in the New National Architecture Manifesto of young militant left-wing architects.

More recently, the semantic dimension inherent in the regionalist approach gained a more precise definition partly owing to the growing interest in conservation. Besides this obvious connection, which also led to a semantic criticism similar to the Italian *criteria semantica* of the early 1960s, more theoretical arguments were also implied.[23] For Turgut Cansever, semantics related to historicity in architecture have a metaphysical significance. They derive from "the unity of forces and the commandments of being [which] determine existence and its continuity."[24] He also calls the communicative ways of this existence and continuity "ornamentality," a concept he advocates.[25] Other theoreticians interpret the same dimension in linguistic and semiotic light and, arguing the fact that "the message is carried by and through codes, and codes themselves are only established through history," again advocate the consideration of "history as a friend." [26]

Functional and programmatic constraints, consumer ideals, social imperatives, leftist criticism, historic and regional advocacies, scientific approaches and positivism in design, rationalist-irrationalist duality, authenticity versus eclectic choice: such are the categories covered by the theoretical and critical debates of the last twenty years. Should one also add some others such as the primacy of technology and the need for adequate design approaches in advanced building systems as it has often been argued?[27] Maybe. More important, however, is the evaluation of the relevance of theory when trying to understand the architectural activity of the period as a whole, especially the artifacts it has produced, buildings and spaces.

This brief outline of the theoretical field shows that the conceptual terminology as well as the operational criteria of architectural criticism were generally imprecise and ambiguous. Despite the large number of buildings which exhibited characteristics belonging to various current international tendencies, the number of critical texts was rather small. Except for the lively debate on regionalism of the early and mid-1960s, appraisals were generally incoherent and subjective. Their subjectivity stemmed not only from their conceptual framework, but also from the lack of theoretical and historical background. Thus, general and vague concepts such as irrationalism were often used in order to set up formal categories.[28] Categories related to intentions, Gestalt principles and details were mixed up; values belonging to different levels of conception and intellectual context were used as equivalents to make value judgments. For instance, a general layout principle such as the "articulated small-block" scheme was used as a counterpart to irrationalism. Although it had been already determined that irrationality should be sought only in a philosophical background which could generate intentions and only subsequently formal configurations, superficial formal features were accepted as sufficient criteria for categorical value judgments.[29]

Unavoidably, the result was imprecise formulations. Since the conceptual categories and criteria were ambiguous, obviously a single building could be assigned to many of these categories at the same time. The Ministry of National Education in Ankara is an example of "irrational" architecture;[30] at the same time we know that it has the "articulated small-block" scheme and a "right-angular" system. Other buildings with the same systems such as the School for Technical Teachers in Ankara were called "rational."[31] But the International Style, which was also "functional", was "rational" too. And obviously the Sheraton Hotel in Istanbul is "irrational," because its scheme is not right-angular (Fig. 83).[32]

This confusion is partly due to the unidimensional nature of the criticism. The absence of any counter-criticism led to a one-way discourse and was exacerbated by the absence of a conceptual framework and a historical tradition of criticism. But even in more fully developed debates, such as in the case of the new regionalism, confusion reigned. Özer was enthusiastic about the Anadolu Club Cafeteria Building in Büyükada by Turgut Cansever for its successful use of the classical T-plan scheme, its integration to the site and its use of raw materials. To him the building was a perfect example of "true regional" (and not regionalist) architecture.[33] Similarly, Kortan's judgment on the Sirer Yalı in Yeniköy by Sedat Eldem paralleled Özer's enthusiasm for the former building.[34] Both buildings possess the characteristics through which Kuban defined new regionalism. Yet, Özer and Kuban did not agree on the theoretical basis of this regionalism.[35]

Later, Özer defended the Tercüman Building in Istanbul, defining it as a successful contemporary interpretation of the classical language (Fig. 104).[36] The Tercüman Building is an extravagant prestige image dangerously forcing the limits of its structural system and having a very poor climatic performance. Can regionality be reduced to planimetric schemes? How can opposing theoreticians agree in one case and disagree in another? Could a thorough and coherent criticism be extracted out of the program for the building? Social criticism tried to answer the last question, but without establishing even a minimal contact with the world and the "life of forms";[37] it saw architecture only as the natural consequence of intentional purposes. This political *prise de position* satisfied itself with condemning or defending ideologies. But it isolated itself from any reference to form, with an ersatz attitude of implicitly assuming that either

Fig. 103 Cansever with Yener, Turkish Historical Society (Türk Tarih Kurumu), Ankara, 1966. (Photo: Christopher Little/Aga Khan Award for Architecture)

Fig. 104 Çilingiroğlu and Tunca, Tercüman Newspaper Offices, Istanbul, 1974. Extreme formal disintegration, the abandonment of raw cement and endless articulation of masses.

ideologies define forms as irreversible processes or that they have no relationship to them. In the first case, we are faced with a naive mechanistic determinism and an ideology which takes on a very dangerous charismatic and totalitarian flavor. In the second, the probable non-coincidence between ideology and architecture cancels any need to introduce an ideological discourse into architectural criticism and thus the case becomes self-contradictory.[38]

Thus it seems that even if an analysis of an architectural criticism and ideologies of these two decades may be helpful in explaining the intellectual atmosphere of the architectural elite, it is generally deceptive and cannot give an understanding of architectural works themselves. Instead of pursuing the metalinguistic discourse of this pioneering criticism, it seems more useful to analyze the architecture itself and its own langue directly: the denotative codes of its architectonic order, and the connotations derived from its referential or significative implications. This will obviously produce another *ex-cathedra* metalinguistic discourse which is the inevitable consequence of any critical analysis that aims to "assume the role of the litmus paper in order to verify the historical validity of architecture."[39]

AN OVERVIEW OF THE ARCHITECTURE

Just as political events are "historical landmarks" which lead to social change, so too in architecture some buildings can be considered as the main turning points of the history of forms. The most important of these pioneer buildings of the 1950s and 1960s were the Sheraton Hotel in Istanbul (Fig. 83), the Karatepe Open Air Museum in Karatepe-Adana (Figs. 97, 98), the Middle East Technical University in Ankara (Fig. 105), the Turkish Historical Society Building in Ankara (Fig. 103), and some early examples of the "articulated small-block" scheme, either designed or built. Yet, old forms continued while new ones were developed. Some buildings designed prior to 1960, such as the DSI Headquarters (Figs. 90, 91), were still under construction and a few new buildings, mostly minor ones, were designed in the International Style. Still others continued to maintain the general lines of the International Style while introducing new

Fig. 105 Çilingiroğlu and Çinici, Middle East Technical University, Faculty of Architecture, Ankara, 1962-1963. Planned along a central axis, the dynamic new university campus utilizes exposed concrete (*beton brut*) extensively. The Faculty of Architecture displays pavilion-type planning and brings in details of the Japanese interpretation of new Brutalism.

concepts. Hukukçular Apartments (Fig. 101) in Istanbul and MTA Buildings (Fig. 106) in Ankara are examples of this latter group.

With their Hukukçular Apartments, Haluk Baysal and Melih Birsel introduced, as it was rightly stressed by Kortan, le Corbusier's *Unité d'Habitation* concept with its morphological elements, the interior street, garden terrace, pilotis.[40] This complex is also important because it introduced a completely new typology into the city's morphic structure. Situated near a boulevard, this new "urban artifact" stands quite independently, breaking the old *rue-corridor* system and realizes the passage *de l'îlot à la barre*, using the very terminology of Castex and Panerai.[41]

The MTA complex of Rahmi Bedir and Demirtaş Kamçıl is more faithful to the Modern Movement tradition. Still, the emphasis on the spaces between its long and low blocs, the concern for scale reflected in their size as well as in the rhythmic modulation of their facades, and the choice of the materials reveal its kinship to newer approaches and render this complex different from orthodox interpretations of the International Style.[42]

Fig. 106 Bediz and Kamçıl, State Mining Institute (MTA) Buildings, Ankara, early 1960s. This is a transitional building between two periods; it accepts the formal geometric order of the International Style but introduces a new morphic expression.

The Distortion of the Right-Angular System

Most critics and architectural historians agree that the Sheraton Hotel in Istanbul is the first example in which "organic" concepts were introduced in the architecture of Turkey (Fig. 83). This building won the first prize in a competition in which Rolf Gutbrod was a jury member. The high block articulates its imposing mass with different orientations, breaking away from the right angular system. The refraction of horizontal geometry confers a rich plasticity, and its planimetry and the vertical elements of its facade support this play of masses and voids. The same multi-directional plasticity is also reflected in the inner space of the lower lobby block. Thus the building is integrated into the city's skyline and at the same time provides a better orientation for the rooms. However, the treatment of surfaces stays plain and simple when compared to a similar hotel scheme in Ankara by Marc Sauger (Fig. 96), where plasticity is accentuated by superficial profiles bringing it closer to kitsch.

A later example of the same aesthetics is the Ministry of Defense Student Dormitories in Tandoğan Square, Ankara, by Şevki Vanlı and Ersen Gömleksizoğlu (Fig. 107). The rectangular geometry of the inner spaces is distorted in the outer envelope; and this plasticity is increased by the accentuation of staircases and of the profiles of the columns. The dramatic dynamism thus gained is transferred to the square on which it stands. Other properties of the same building such as the organization of the students' rooms around central halls relate the planimetry to traditional or archetypal references.[43]

Fig. 107 Vanlı and Gömleksizoğlu, Ministry of Defense Student Dormitories, Ankara, 1967-1968. Dormitories accommodate students whose parents are Ministry of Defense personnel.

These works have somewhat of a Wrightian plasticity, but other designs which used polyangular patterns were akin to German *Organhaft* conceptions. However, the latter approach, apparent in the Turkish Pavilion design for the New York World's Fair of 1964 by Ruşen Dora and Ünal Demiraslan, had few successors.[44] Perhaps the major example was the Istanbul Congress Palace by Somer Ural and Oktay Gürün, designed in the late 1960s, still under construction. However, it has been altered drastically from its original design.

The absence in these schemes of any reference to an irrationalist philosophy which an authentic *Organhaft* design should possess is perhaps one reason for the small number of these works.[45] Another would be the high performance and sophistication of building craft which the realization of an authentic *Organhaft* design required. Given the technological and economic state of Turkey's building industry, such standards were difficult to achieve.

Wright, Scharoun and why not Aalto? The pursuit for new formal expression within a pluralism of influences could hardly avoid the soft expression achieved by the sinuous plasticity of the Finnish master. The distortion of the canonical prism of the 1950s finally resulted in the undulations of raw brick or visible cement surfaces. An obvious example is the Auditorium of the Middle East Technical University by Altuğ and Behruz Çinici (Fig. 108). The Istanbul University Central Library by Sevinç and Şandor Hadi and Hüseyin Başçetinçelik is close in general conception to Aalto's Wolfsburg Cultural Center (Fig. 109). Whatever the source of inspiration, breaking away from the rigid geometry imposed by a monolithic morphic grammar allowed Turkish architects a more dramatic and softer expression achievable not only in monumental but also in smaller buildings. Nezih Eldem's apartment building in Arifipaşa Korusu, Istanbul, with the faceted orientation of its units, the Italianizing inner street between the blocs and a functional and plastic integration into the topography, is one example (Fig. 110). In the Türker Villa in Adana by Şevki Vanlı, the inner space is organized around a court element, perpetuating a traditional spatial order, and is sheltered by inclined roof surfaces in a simple, oblique geometry (Fig. 111). Both buildings were

Fig. 108 Çinici and Çinici, Middle East Technical University Auditorium, Ankara.

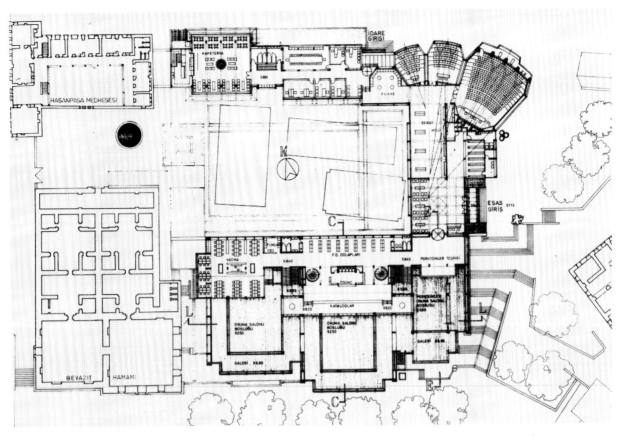

completed in the 1960s. An earlier example is the Dumlupınar Monument by Levent Aksüt and Yaşar Marulyalı, in which tension is created by modest triangular elements and which has a dramatic monumentality achieved not only by the integral plasticity of the masses but also by the dynamics of the space surrounding them.

Fig. 109 Hadi, Hadi and Başçetinçelik, Istanbul University Central Library, Istanbul, 1964-1981.

Fig. 110 Eldem, Nezih, Apartments, Istanbul, 1960s.

Fig. 111 Vanlı, Türker Villa, Adana, 1960s.

The Disaggregation of the Prism: Articulated Small Blocks Scheme and the New Brutalist Ethics

To complete the destruction of the sacred prism, a final step was necessary. The prism realized within the limitations of its own geometry was divided into the smaller parts, perpetuating the geometric order of the whole and establishing a hierarchy of size of the new volumes thus constituted. Quoting Benedikt Huber, Özer calls this "gradual additive system" (*das Additive durch Staffeln*) a "composition of simple geometrical masses in order to create a small and piecemeal (*klein und vielteilig*) order."[46] According to the latter, this tendency allows for free forms while remaining "rationalist." Such a tendency is common in many Western designs of the early 1960s, such as Van den Broek and Bakema's Marl project and Utzon's Helsingor housing group. Later, Kortan established the common characteristics of this new solution in their compositional, functional, expressive, topographical and formal features.[47] He also analyzes several layouts proposed in Turkish architectural competitions of the early 1960s and develops a systematic criticism. According to him, this approach lacks flexibility and growth potential; the solutions are generally incompatible with rational building techniques such as standardization and modular coordination; and their overall application in different climatological and functional contexts calls for a more careful consideration of the conditions, which he finds closer in planimetric configuration to some Mondrian or other supermatist paintings.[48]

Fig. 112 Tekeli, Sisa and Hepgüler, Complex of Retail Shops (Manifaturacılar Çarşısı), Istanbul, 1959. Detail of an internal courtyard.

This approach produced many buildings for over a decade, and it also influenced further developments. Two earlier examples were Manifaturacılar Çarşısı in Istanbul (Figs. 5, 100) and the Antalya Museum by the Tekeli-Sisa-Hepgüler group. In both cases, keeping the buildings in the right scale with their neighborhood was a programmatic prerequisite. And the articulated small blocks scheme was found to be a suitable solution. In their shopping complex the architects attempted to create a residential area pattern. Small blocs are arranged around open spaces, squares and axes; a vertical circulation system is incorporated into the different levels of the platforms which house groups of shops (Fig. 112). Flat roofs of different levels accentuate the horizontality of the simple lines of floors; a red grid of trellises, used for shading, completes the piecemeal small scale of the complex in order to integrate it to the surrounding old wooden houses of the historic Süleymaniye district. But the functional purpose of the retail center has always remained incompatible with the aims of such an environment-conscious design program.

Several other designs of the same basic scheme proliferated from 1965 to 1970. The Agricultural Products Office by Vedat Özsan, Cengiz Bektaş, Oral Vural; and the Directorate of State Highways by Aktan Okan and Fikret Cankut, including the addition of a Guest Center by Oral Vural, and the METU Faculty of Architecture (Fig. 105) are examples of that scheme.

In all these buildings there exists a dualism between the free articulation of volumes and the conventional interpretation of surfaces of the old International Style. Also apparent is another influence which brings a certain coherence to this style. That is the so-called New Brutalism. The term obviously has different references;[49] but at least in the Turkish case, one can refer to Team 10, Kahn and Japanese inspirations and perhaps the Swiss Atelier 5 Group. Whatever the specific sources, Brutalist characteristics in the realizations of forms were obvious. The use of raw

Fig. 113 Özsan, Bektaş and Vural, Agricultural Products Office (TMO) Headquarters, Ankara, 1964.

materials, the volumetric accentuation of functional spaces and elements as well as some technical devices and the refutation of preconceived formal solutions were the most apparent. It can be argued that such a formal realization was a natural evolution of the small articulated blocks scheme.

The new aesthetics can be seen in many buildings. The construction of the new Middle East Technical University allowed a gathering of inspirations. During more than ten years of its construction, Behruz and Altuğ Çinici built an amalgam of forms borrowed from different sources. Japan, Aalto, Bakema, Rudolph, Gowan and Stirling, and finally Anatolian culture were brought together, interpreted, and recomposed with the touch of a talent. The syncretic result is obviously open to criticism. But the merits of this first large-scale realization and its formal impact on later developments are notable.

With the Brutalist reinterpretation of the articulated small blocks scheme, mass was reintroduced into Turkish architecture. Architectonic mass was no longer reduced to the fragile horizontal and vertical lines of the orthogonal grid of Modern Movement facades. It gained an autonomous expression in the volumetric appearance of the raw surfaces: staircases, building parts, etc. were often pierced with small holes only. The new expression is apparent in the volumetric order of the Anadolu Club in Ankara by Ertur Yener (Fig. 114).

The use of raw cement surfaces accentuated volumetric expression and became a basic aesthetic element in the above-mentioned METU Faculty of Architecture, the Stad Hotel in Ankara by the Tekeli-Sisa-Hepgüler group (Fig. 115); the small apartment bloc in Göztepe, Istanbul, by Mehmet Konuralp (Fig. 116) and the Karadeniz Technical University Sports Hall and Auditorium in Trabzon by Erkut Şahinbaş. In the Stad Hotel, a more dramatic expression was achieved through the combination of articulated masses and voids by the use of raw surfaces and also by the verticality of high-rise monobloc volumes.

Fig. 114 Yener, Anadolu Club, Ankara, 1962-1965.

Fig. 116 Konuralp, Apartments, Göztepe, Istanbul, 1974.

The extreme articulation of parts was another expressive system. The best examples are the work of Günay Çilingiroğlu and Muhlis Tunca, first in their Istanbul Reklam Building and then in other ones. In the first case, their building surrounds a small historic building, without touching it. The small volumes connect with hollow intersection details; structural elements are apparent. The final expression is a sculptured, "dematerialized," tiny membrane which embraces the outer space more than its own inner space. In the Tercüman building, this expressive search has reached the limits of interpretation (Fig. 104). An archetypal scheme borrowed from a traditional Turkish house has been adopted for the plan of a building designed for a major Istanbul daily. However, the basic scheme is over-articulated. The "inflation" of the inner space, which is apparent in the audacious cantilever of the main floor, disintegrates the volumes. Standing outside the dense urban center, the building is a landmark for a commercialism seen only from a main highway. The strong plastic expression is accentuated by the verticality of inner corner towers. Syntactic decomposition to such an extreme also disaggregates the meanings which such a syntax carried with it. What then is the remaining semantic output of its archetypal reference? If one thing is clear, it is that such a "post-Brutalist" over-articulation creates a paradoxical monumentality through extreme interplay between its dematerialized masses and the outer space they so powerfully define.

Fig. 115 Tekeli and Sisa, Stad Hotel, Ankara, 1965-1970.

Fig. 117 Çilingiroğlu and Tunca, Istanbul Reklâm Building, Istanbul, 1965-1969.

Fig. 118 Sargın and Böke, Iş Bankası Tower, Ankara, 1976.

Fig. 119 Tecimen, Odakule Center, Istanbul. Designed and built in the 1970s for the Chamber of Industry.

New Monumentality and Symbolism

Thus symbolism and monumentality appeared on the horizon of Turkish architecture, not only in such disarticulated schemes but in large and compact blocs. Either high-rise or horizontally developed, these buildings attained a singular expression through the unity of their form. This singularity associated with the imposing size of the buildings creates a monumentality which very often carries symbolic connotations. Most of these realizations call for very advanced technologies and a perfection in details. They can only appear at a more developed stage of the national economy and of the building industry. Frequently, very expensive building materials were also used in these ambitious buildings which were generally financed by big business.

The best examples are by the Iş Bankası Tower in Ankara and its minor counterparts in Istanbul, Odakule and the State Highways Buildings. The Iş Bankası Tower, a monumental landmark not constrained by a dense urban environment (Fig. 118). Odakule, on the other hand, creates a rupture in the continuation of a strong historical linear pattern of Istiklâl Caddesi (Fig. 119). Other designs such as the Council of State in Ankara by

Fig. 120 Eldem, Akbank, Fındıklı, Istanbul. A simplified classicism confers monumentality to this small-scale office building of the 1970s.

Fig. 121 Bektaş, Turkish Language Society (Türk Dil Kurumu), Ankara, 1972-1978.

Fig. 122 Bektaş, Turkish Language Society (Türk Dil Kurumu), Ankara, 1972-1978. Detail of the staircase block.

Tekeli and Sisa and the National Library in Ankara by the Ministry of Public Works team also constitute examples of compactness in grand scale, with more or less symbolic impact.

A final example is the Lassa Tire Factory in Adapazarı by Tekeli and Sisa (Fig. 6). Obviously, the industrial activity involved confers an immediate functional basis for the form generation of factory buildings. However, the compactness of the monobloc mass, the explicit choice apparent in formal configurations such as the curvilinear contours of the modular units and the shape of the round window holes (scuttles), give a monumentality and assign an industrial symbolism to this building.

A characteristic of these imposing compact masses is their finite unity, regardless of their neighboring elements. These buildings attain monumentality not only through their dimensions, but perhaps more so through their "just standing there." That is, they only exist *per se*; and this "being there" is what confers an inherent monumentality to them.[50] It is the same reason that smaller buildings, even when situated within an existing context, assume a similar monumentality. Such is the case with Sedat Eldem's Akbank in Fındıklı, Istanbul, with its simple facade of a vertical salient collonade (Fig. 20). The repetition of a series of double vertical windows is associated with this static order.[51] And the result is a classical monumental expression without any mannerist ornament in a modest office building.

A similar example is Cengiz Bektaş's Turkish Language Society in Ankara (Fig. 121). As early as 1970, before its construction, Bektaş had expressed his admiration for Eldem's building.[52] Bektaş's building, however, differs in several aspects from the former. With its articulation of the staircase bloc, with the angular position of its corner columns and the difference in the vertical line of its windows, this building is more in scale with the neighboring street space (Fig. 122). But the unity of expression, in volume as well as in the central inner space, gives it a singular monumentality, and a symbolic impact.[53]

Fig. 123 Özsan, Apartment, Çankaya, Ankara, mid-1970s.

Search for a Historical Basis

Between these two opposite tendencies, the articulation of fragmented small blocs and the compactness in grand scale, a third one emerged. It was to be the basis for a series of buildings successfully integrated into existing urban fabrics. On small urban plots where no big masses were allowed, articulation was realized on the facade, or in the spatial order, or both, through alternate planimetric typologies. And where larger volumetric freedom was no longer possible, diversity was sought in the richness of semantic references. Obviously, these realizations are modest: they cannot attain the grandeur of a symphony but rather are *kleine Musik* pieces. They have a convenient and coherent vocabulary which relates them to the historic milieu in which they are located. This is realized by some morphic elements, or arrangements: profiles, window shapes, facade organizations, roof edges, even color choices. The latter produced Cansever's "ornamentality" effect. While there is no overall canon for harmony, the scale and the relevance of the connotations are important.[54]

Several buildings can be mentioned. An earlier example is the apartment house in Çankaya, Ankara, by Vedat Özsan in which the articulation of two rectangular blocs is adjusted perfectly to a corner plot (Fig. 123). In the Central Bank (Merkez Bankası) in Bursa, Şevki Vanlı and Ersen

Fig. 124 Elmas, Yener and Gülçur, Vakıflar Bankası, Ankara, 1974-1978.

Fig. 125 Giray and Nezih Eldem, Agricultural Bank Extension (Ziraat Bankası), Istanbul.

Gömleksizoğlu realized an articulated facade through angular profiles. By playing with the vertical expression of the facade, they reflected the different functions of the floors, a solution which helped them to scale the entire volume. Varied functions such as offices and residential units on different floors always yielded interesting patterns, reminiscent of the well-known Passarelli Building in Rome.

In the earlier Pamukbank and the later Hisarbank, both in Istanbul, Tekeli and Sisa also produced soft, ornamented, "in-scale" architecture. Cengiz Bektaş in the Central Bank at Denizli was trying for the same effect as were Erdoğan Elmas, Ertur Yener and Zafer Gülçur in the Vakıflar Bankası of Ankara but with more reference to classical Ottoman forms (Fig. 124). Muhteşem Giray and Nezih Eldem's Ziraat Bankası extension in Karaköy, Istanbul, attempts to harmonize with an existing building by establishing simultaneous continuities of surfaces and textures and discontinuities of window arrangements (Fig. 125). This play is seen in Nezih Eldem's and Atilla Yücel's Istanbul University Academic Center project, in which cantilevered upper floors on different levels produce a soft plasticity. One can also cite Arolat's office building in Osmanbey, Istanbul, in which the ornamented profile of the fluted circular columns contrasts with the silent response of reflecting colored window frames. Thus, despite the continuity of its convex surface, the building articulates the outer space of the intersecting roads. The project of Alpay Aşkun and Ilgi Yüce for the Government Offices at Afyon is another example of successful integration into the environment. In this example, a rather expressionist solid mass is articulated around a preserved building, thus creating a dramatic duality.

Consciousness for scale and city sense are concepts akin to historicity. And history has been the immutable axis on and around which theoretical architectural debates have focused in the last decades. As it was in many other parts of the world, in Turkey too, a stream of certain "passéism" has been felt in architecture since the early 1960s. The case was described by Zevi, who was arguing in 1963: "Saturated with technology and rational objectivism, the architects were again oriented to tradition; they were influenced by existing environments, took antique examples of their buildings, but with a disarming superficiality...."[55] And the case was not limited to architecture. In music, much of contemporary Turkish poliphony has followed Bela Bartok's or Zoltan Kodaly's aesthetics. In poetry, in which a rich tradition exists, after more than twenty years of constructivism, dada, surrealism, abstract formalism and obscurantism, there was a return to realism, often combined with allusions to traditional poetry, even to the rejected Ottoman high tradition.[56]

New regionalism was contemporaneous to these developments. The Karatepe Open Air Museum (Figs. 97, 98) by Turgut Cansever was an early example, and the shape of the elegant raw concrete shelters soon became a prototype for reinterpretations of traditional forms. The roof forms were combined with other local elements such as corner windows and covered balconies (*cumba*) and were constructed through the use of rationalized traditional *in-situ* building techniques. These forms and procedures were used by Ertur Yener in his Cafeteria Building in Büyükada, associated with a classical T-plan; again by Turgut Cansever in his articulated apartment blocs in Çiftehavuzlar, Istanbul; and were further developed by the latter in his partly realized Terakki Foundation School project in Istanbul.[57]

The more sophisticated examples of the new re-historicized architecture are two buildings by two of its leading proponents, Turgut Cansever and Sedat Eldem: the Turkish Historical Society in Ankara,[58] and the Social Security Complex (SSK) in Istanbul. From the exterior, the Historical Society Building of Cansever and Ertur Yener has a defensive character, a fortress paradoxically with an overhang on pilotis (Fig. 103). All the interior space and activities are grouped and organized around a three-storey covered atrium; the scheme thus refers to the Ottoman *medrese* (Fig. 126). Carefully controlled light is a very important element in this introverted spatial order, since the central space is treated as the counterpart of an outer, urban space: a square, with all the activities concentrated around it (Fig. 127). Zenithal light becomes an architectonic element, distributed through interior *kafeses, mashrabiyya* trellises (another metaphoric use of a traditional facade element), and by the roof lanterns which accentuate the fortress image, and unavoidably, the imposing Ankara fortress. Surrounding forms, mainly the monumental Faculty of Language, Geography and History by Bruno Taut, are also acknowledged in the choice of the materials: reddish Ankara stone in the heavy mass of the cantilevered upper walls and painted raw cement in lower structural elements. These elements are projected into the facade and support the heavy mass "like the fingers of a hand." Thus, Cansever and Yener produce a spatial order full of historical, environmental and behavioral connotations, using an ornamented, metaphoric vocabulary, organized around a basic archetypal syntax. Their building "talks" about architecture through its architectonics. And far from being a simple artifact, the architecture thus becomes a discourse (Fig. 128).

Fig. 126 Cansever with Yener, Turkish Historical Society, Ankara, 1966. Atrium. (Photo: Christopher Little/Aga Khan Award for Architecture)

Fig. 127 Cansever with Yener, Turkish Historical Society, Ankara, 1966. Detail of interior *kafes*es, *mashrabiyya* trellises and roof lanterns. (Photo: Christopher Little/Aga Khan Award for Architecture)

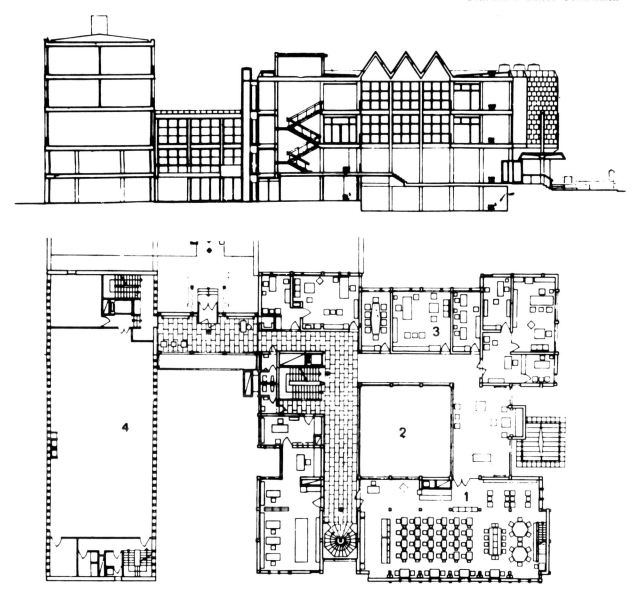

In the Social Security Complex, located in the historical Zeyrek district of Istanbul, connotations are more direct and less frequent. Here, Eldem proposes an extension of the existing historic Zeyrek quarter. The building complex exactly reproduces the basic pattern of an urban residential aggregate, with the small blocs articulated around narrow open spaces: streets, by-passes and squares (Fig. 129). The blocs of different levels each repeat common facade elements: rows of vertical windows modulated by small columns, the gradual projection of upper floors, flat roofs with salient, tiny edge profiles, an atomized small-scale impression, accentuated by the use of geometrically ornamented panels on the surfaces (Fig. 130). This architecture stands in between the spatial morphology of a spontaneous historic Istanbul quarter and the rigid discipline of an August Perret classicism.

Fig. 128 Cansever with Yener, Turkish Historical Society, Ankara, 1966. Plan and section.

Fig. 129 Eldem, Social Security Complex (SSK), Istanbul, 1963-1970.

Fig. 130 Eldem, Social Security Complex, Istanbul, 1963-1970. Corbels, cantilevers, eaves and sun shades are referents to the past architecture within a modern structure.

Both buildings have been highly influential on later architecture. An interpretation of the Historical Society introversion reappears in the volumetric order of the Istanbul University Library (Fig. 131). The vertical-horizontal duality of the Zeyrek complex and its facade treatment were repeated by Eldem in his small Sirer Yalı in Yeniköy, Istanbul, with the salient flat roof element, and its double balconies, each modulated differently by the "hanging columns" of the facade. They were to be reinterpreted in Erdoğan Elmas's Cavcav Villa in Ankara and even in Cansever's small Nadaroğlu House in Burgaz, Istanbul. A closer reinterpretation of the Social Security Complex aesthetics is seen in several small-scale Istanbul buildings, such as the Ziraat Bankası in Bakırköy by Maruf Önal.

The reference to an old tradition, either interpreting its syntax or reproducing the elements of its vocabulary, implies a metaphoric use. This fact is well stressed by Bonta, who states: "Abandoning a form ... is a rare event in the history of design. Once a form is established and has become familiar to a certain community, it will tend to recur over and over again before fading, 're-semanticized' with some subtle principle of economy. Changes of meaning are far more frequent than the disappearance of forms."[59] This statement recalls Eco's concept of "code" being formed throughout history[60] and Mukařovský's determination of artistic "functions." It also implies "historical sets of forms," based on "preexisting codes,"[61] and gives the axial articulation of any theoretical discourse on

historicity and regionality in architecture. In addition to the examples discussed, series of buildings in other regional contexts give a rich basis for such a critical analysis.

During the years of construction of the Karatepe Museum, Cansever and Yener proposed a scheme based on blocs and groups organized around courtyards for the competition of a High School building in Diyarbakır, a town in hot and arid southwest Anatolia. This project won the competition, but has remained unrealized. However, its impact can be discerned. More than ten years later, the Aru Group won the competition for the University of Diyarbakır, proposing a more rigid and geometrical version of a similar, climatically adapted scheme of the courtyard pattern as a solution for regional conditions. More obvious examples of regionalism can be seen in many of the large resort villages, either projected or built on the Mediterranean and Aegean coasts; they generally reproduce the spatial pattern as well as the forms, and in some cases even the building techniques of the indigenous architecture. However, the functional use is different; several nuances of formal sources coexist and very often the construction system and some materials are also imported. Where roof terraces are expensive with new building techniques, an alternative *ersatz* use of another local form, the pitched roof, is available. These tendencies are apparent in the Datça and Bodrum holiday villages by the EPA Group (Fig. 132), and in the Kemer holiday village (Club Méditerranée) by Tuncay Çavdar and Giorgio Giovannini (Fig. 133). In the Artur resort village in Edremit and especially Yüksel village in Güllük, Altuğ and Behruz Çinici have brought free interpretations and even more fantasy to the eclecticism of the former examples (Fig. 134).

The transfer of vernacular forms from their authentic regional context to new usages through some formal or structural shifting again raises the question of the re-semanticization of the code. What are the very meanings that such a re-semanticized new code carries? Are they more related to the regional conditions, or to consumption and prestige ideals? In their stimulating research on the new French regional Provençal architecture, Sylvia Ostrowetsky and Samuel Bordreuil have argued the second case.

Fig. 131 Hadi, Hadi and Başçetinçelik, Istanbul University Central Library, Istanbul, 1964-1981.

Fig. 132 EPA Group, Gürsel, Çubuk, Güner, Holiday Village, Bodrum, 1970s.

Fig. 133 Çavdar, Giovannini and Giovannini, Holiday Village (Club Méditerrannée), Kemer.

Fig. 134 Çinici and Çinici, Yüksel Village, Güllük, 1970s.

And then, the discourse on the relevance of this metaphoric semanticism in architecture assumes moral dimensions.

Whatever the answers advocated by this criticism to such an ethical issue may be, the analysis of the architectural production shows that different architectural orientations were adopted by Turkish designers in order to give positive answers for current historical/regional alternatives:

a) The most favorable attitude is the acceptance of the formal elements as they are. This was the implicit answer given by the architects of many resort villages and vacation houses. One of the best and most moderate examples is by Behruz Çinici in the brick architecture of his faculty housing on METU campus. Whether one calls this attitude new-regional, pseudo-vernacular, or eclectic-folkloristic, one characteristic is clear: it accepts traditional architecture and different subcultures within it as a repertory of forms, open to a large choice and even a combinatory usage of them, exactly as the usage made in the eighteenth century of the generative typology proposed by Durand.[62]

b) Eldem's attitude of a rational architectonic interpretation of the traditional form is a second alternative. Except in his SSK Zeyrek project, in which more importance is accorded to the environment and scale, Eldem subjects a given, seldom historical, form to a clinical architectonic

Fig. 135 Eldem, Suna Koç Yalı, Istanbul, early 1970s.

analysis. The basic typology and the context-free syntax remain unchanged, while a new techtonic order is reconstituted by the use of new materials and the influence of new usage and aesthetics. But a more important feature is the consideration of the building as a static object, exactly as is the case of compact grand-scale buildings. And these realizations— houses, *yalıs*, embassies—are classic, not only because of their forms or symmetry, but merely because they are, independently of their real size, monumental and atemporal (Fig. 135).

c) The deeper philosophical interpretation of Cansever is a third example. Here, not only the abstract form is considered, but also the space and its existential meanings are discussed. The unity or diversity of these references have no prime importance, since the resulting formal configuration is unique. Sedat Eldem in his Zeyrek project, Nezih Eldem in the Istanbul Military Museum and to some extent Behruz Çinici in his Public Relations Offices building of the National Assembly in Ankara, share the same approach which Cansever pursues to an extreme in his proposal for the Atatürk Cultural Center in Ankara (Fig. 136). In this example, a complex and dissonant syntax is established, using a diversity of references, Anatolian and Ottoman subcultures, Iranian schemes, his own work, and a reference to the city of Ankara, a large horizontal element as a response to the piecemeal fabric of the town. Thus, not only the formal elements, but the entire scheme becomes "ornamented by connotative references."

d) The final alternative is the free formal interpretations of Behruz Çinici who, starting from either context-related or arbitrary references, uses these elements in a series of perpetual formal configurations. The form is neither used as it is, nor re-semanticized, but remodeled in itself. The result is a rich, somewhat fantastic deformation of the initial form. Some examples are the Güllük project for a Residential Complex for Libyan Army Officers to be built in Tripoli.

Outside of these categories, only two other trends exist: complete anti-historicism and the pastiche. In these cases, architecture remains either

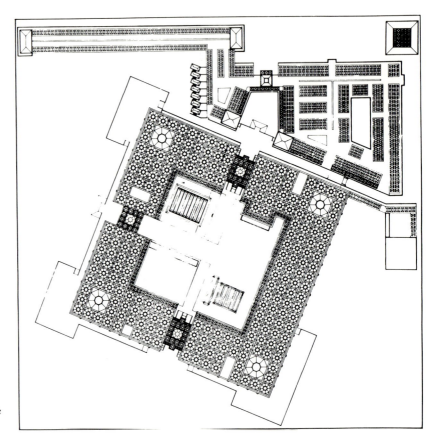

Fig. 136 Cansever, Project for the Atatürk Cultural Center, Ankara.

reduced to a tool-object, or its meanings are totally mercantilized. And both approaches mean the negation of any coherent historical dimension.

FINAL REMARKS

Some important activities affecting architecture and built environment have not been included in this essay. These are activities related to conservation and rehabilitation as well as those involved with advanced building technologies and industrial buildings. Since our discussion was focused on the new architecture in Turkey rather than the development of the physical environment, no reference was made to conservation.

As for advanced building technologies, their efficient and broad usage was only reflected in industrial buildings, the above-mentioned Lassa factory being the best example (Figs. 6, 138). Other important works are, in chronological order: the Arçelik and Ipek paper plants by Aydın Boysan, the FIAT-TOFAŞ Factory by Metin Hepgüler, the OYAK-Renault Factory by Tekeli and Sisa, and the Istanbul-Yeşilköy Air Terminal Buildings by Hayati Tabanlıoğlu, now under construction. However, the efficient use of industrialized building techniques applied in industrial buildings has not yet been transferred to large-scale mass housing, the most important area of potential application.

The diversity of tendencies of the last two decades shows that pluralism has been the only suitable common denominator for architecture as a cultural product, whether in theory or in practice. If the art of architecture

Fig. 137 Çinici and Çinici, Iranian Primary School, Ankara. This building is an addition to the existing Iranian Cultural Center by Aptullah Kuran.

Fig. 138 Tekeli and Sisa, Lassa Tire Factory, Izmit, 1975-1977.

is a mirror, it only reflected a pluralistic atmosphere, and not its individual elements. And if it is a lamp, the light it shed was not bright enough to produce a unique environmental quality, a common taste; such an environmental unity would be nonsense, especially in the absence of a unified strategy for urban mass housing.

A rich mix of thoughts, tendencies, processes and end-products were realized in this pluralistic milieu. All were somewhat fragmentary, with no coherent links between theory and criticism, context and end-product. However, if in such a syncretic and chaotic milieu, deprived of deep beliefs and value systems, the artistic creation could not fit the reality delineated by theory and social criticism, it produced a kind of "co-reality," [63] and yet this co-reality is closely related to history. All the artistic creation of the period oscillates between innovation and history.

NOTES

1. "1970'te Mimarimiz," *Mimarlık* (Architecture) 12 (December, 1970).

2. See Chapter I.

3. *Ibid.* For a general analysis of the 1960-1970 period, see also S. Yerasimos, *Azgelişmişlik Sürecinde Türkiye* (Turkey: A Case of Underdevelopment), vol. III (Istanbul, 1976); Y. Küçük, *Planlama, Kalkınma ve Türkiye* (Planning, Development and Turkey) (Istanbul, 1971).

4. The importance of their influence has been stressed by several critics. Cf. B. Özer, *Rejyonalizm, Üniversalizm ve Çağdaş Mimarimiz Üzerine Bir Deneme* (An Essay on Regionalism, Universalism and Our Contemporary Architecture) (Istanbul, 1964), 6.2.7; E. Kortan, *Türkiye'de Mimarlık Hareketleri ve Eleştirisi: 1960-1970* (Architectural Movements in Turkey and Their Criticism: 1960-1970), Chapter III; Ü. Alsaç, "Türk Mimarlık Düşüncesinin Cumhuriyet Devrindeki Evrimi" (The Evolution of Turkish Architectural Thought during the Republican Period) *Mimarlık* 11-12 (November-December, 1973).

5. See *Mimarlık* 12 (December, 1972): special issue on architectural education; Ü. Alsaç, "Türk Mimarlık Düşüncesi," p. 18.

6. The following figures illustrate the increasing number of architects. In 1950 there were fewer than 400 architects; in 1960 fewer than 900; in 1970 fewer than 4000, but in 1980 over 10,000 (Source: Turkish Chamber of Architects).

7. For a detailed, analytical treatment, see Türkiye Mühendisler ve Mimarlar Odaları Birliği, *Mühendisler, Mimarlar* (Engineers, Architects) (Istanbul, 1978).

8. *Ibid.* is the best example of this ambiguous bipolarity; see also S. Ural and H. Çakır, *Yeni Ulusal Mimarlık* (New National Architecture) (Istanbul, 1971).

9. The theory of architecture has recently been treated in reviews and articles by S. Dostoğlu, H. Ertekin and A. Yücel published in *Mimarlık* since 1979.

10. B. Zevi's ideas were first introduced in Turkey by B. Özer, "Bir Kitap Özeti: Bruno Zevi, *Saper Vedere l'Architettura,*" *Mimarlık ve Sanat* no. 2 (1961). The *Organhaft* theories were widely discussed in special lectures by H.K. Söylemezoğlu, E. Aksoy, B. Özer, and J. Joedicke at the Istanbul Technical University.

11. Özer, *Rejyonalizm*, p. 80.

12. *Ibid.*, p. 81.

13. B. Özer, "Mimaride Üslûp, Batı ve Biz" (Style in Architecture: the West and Us) *Mimarlık* 11 (November, 1965), p. 28; reprinted in B. Özer, *Bakışlar* (Views) (Istanbul, 1969).

14. Among those can be mentioned E. Kortan, *Türkiye'de Mimarlık Hareketleri*; M. Tapan and M. Sözen, *Elli Yılın Türk Mimarisi* (Fifty Years of Turkish Architecture) (Istanbul, 1973).

15. Alsaç, "Türk Mimarlık Düşüncesi," p. 18.

16. This terminology has been widely and uniformly used by Turkish critics, particularly by Özer and Kortan.

17. Alsaç, "Türk Mimarlık Düşüncesi," p. 18.

18. Kortan, *Türkiye'de Mimarlık Hareketleri*, p. 79.

19. D. Kuban, "Bizde Rejyonalizm Üzerine" (On Regionalism in Turkey) *Mimarlık ve Sanat* no. 1 (1961), pp. 14-15.

20. D. Kuban, "Modern Mimarinin Gerçek Yolu" (The True Path of Modern Architecture) *Mimarlık ve Sanat* no. 2 (1961).

21. B. Özer, *Rejyonalizm*, 6.2, argues for an architecture which "comes from us and which is our own, yet not regionalist but really regional." According to him, this type of architecture differs from an artificial adaptation of forms because it is geared to actual conditions.

22. S.H. Eldem, "Toward a Local Idiom: A Summary History of Contemporary Architecture in Turkey," R. Holod, ed., *Conservation as Cutural Survival* (Philadelphia, 1980). See also S.H. Eldem, "Elli Yıllık Cumhuriyet Mimarlığı" (Fifty Years of Republican Architecture) *Mimarlık* 11-12 (November-December, 1973), pp. 5-11.

23. This type of criticism is to be found in the works of S. Bettini, I. Gamberini and G. Klaus-Koenig.

24. T. Cansever, *Thoughts and Architecture* (Ankara, 1981), p. 8.

25. T. Cansever, "Mimarlıkta Tezyinilik" (Decoration in Architecture): paper presented at the ÇEMBIL Conference, Ankara, 1979.

26. A. Yücel, *Mimarlıkta Biçim ve Mekânın Dilsel Yorumu Üzerine* (On the Linguistic Interpretation of Form and Space in Architecture) (Ankara, forthcoming), discusses these issues in reference to the work of U. Eco and P. Porthoghesi.

27. Several authors stressed the importance attached to technology in the answers given to the above-mentioned questionnaire distributed by *Mimarlık*: cf. A. Boysan, *Mimarlık* 12 (December, 1970).

28. It is clear that when rationalism (or irrationalism) is used in its historical/philosophical idiomatic context, no semantic ambiguity remains. Ambiguity begins when formal features are taken as sufficient criteria for considering a building as being rationalist or irrationalist without any reference to historical explanation. And this value judgment remains vague since features of form such as angular or circular configuration can also be products of strict rationalism without any subjective or "irrational"s intention.

29. Özer, "Mimaride Üslûp," p. 23; *idem*, "Ifade Çeşitliliği Yönünden Çağdaş Mimariye Bir Bakış" (Contemporary Architecture from the Viewpoint of Variety of Expression) *Mimarlık* 3 (March, 1967), pp. 13-42.

30. Kortan, *Türkiye'de Mimarlık Hareketleri*, pp. 137-139.

31. Özer, *Rejyonalizm*, p. 77.

32. *Ibid.*, pp. 76-77; see also Kortan, *Türkiye'de Mimarlık Hareketleri*, pp. 120-121.

33. B. Özer, "T Planı ve Çağdaş Mimarimiz" (T-Plan and Our Contemporary Architecture); and also anonymous review in *Mimarlık* 12 (December, 1966).

34. Kortan, *Türkiye'de Mimarlık HareketlerI*, pp. 118-119.

35. Cf. nn. 11, 13, 19, 20, above.

36. B. Özer, comment made at the Seminar on Gelenekselle Yaşama ve Yeniden Inşa Etme (Living with the Traditional and Rebuilding), Academy of Fine Arts, Istanbul, 1978.

37. The reference made implies the entire content of H. Focillon, *Vie des formes*, 3rd ed. (Paris, 1947).

38. Self-contradiction is obviously valid in such a categorical critical stance. In another theoretical approach, articulated best by Aldo Rossi, the logical conflict disappears. However, the absolute arbitrariness of the relations between ideology and form also invokes extremely antagonistic theoretical attitudes, such as those of Tafuri and Maldonado. Cf. T. Maldonado, *La Speranza Progettuale* (Torino, 1970) and M. Tafuri, *Progetto e Utopia* (Bari, 1973).

39. M. Tafuri, *Teorie e Storia dell'Architettura* (Bari, 1973), p. 270.

40. Kortan, *Türkiye'de Mimarlık Hareketleri*, pp. 97-98.

41. Cf. J. Castex, J-Ch. Depaule, P. Panerai, *De l'Ilot à la barre* (Paris, 1975). The issue brings to mind all the Italian and French discourse on typology/morphology relations. For a Turkish treatment, see A. Yücel, "Mimarlıkta Tipoloji Kavramları" (Concepts of Typology in Architecture) *ITÜYAK Bülteni* 2 (1977).

42. Kortan finds the interpretation of the building materials by Bediz and Kamçıl close to the new brutalist ethics: cf. Kortan, *Türkiye'de Mimarlık Hareketleri*, pp. 99-101.

43. See the statements quoted in Ş. Vanlı, *Mimarlık 12 (December, 1970), pp. 50-51.*

44. *Özer, Rejyonalizm, p. 77,* related this design to Sharoun and called it "irrational"; but Kortan, *Türkiye'de Mimarlık Hareketleri*, p. 140, defined it as "mannerist."

45. By "irrational philosophy" is meant a metaphysical though theosophical system such as

that of Rudolf Steiner. Our definition is also close to the irrationalism inherent in the philosophy of a "Glass Chain" group.

46. Özer, *Rejyonalizm*.

47. Kortan, *Türkiye'de Mimarlık Hareketleri*, p. 70.

48. *Ibid.*, pp. 78-80.

49. See R. Banham, *The New Brutalism* (New York, 1966). On New Brutalist aesthetics, see K. Frampton, *Modern Architecture* (London, 1968), Part III, Chapter 2, where relations between New Brutalism and Palladianism, humanism, "formalism," and "populism" are discussed. Alsaç implies a relationship between New Brutalist aesthetics and regional culture: see n. 15, above. The first systematic analysis in Turkey of New Brutalism was made in the lectures by J. Joedicke, Istanbul Technical University, 1964; published in B. Özer and O. Göçer, eds., *Modern Mimarinin Gelişimi* (The Development of Modern Architecture) (Istanbul, 1966), pp. 147-163.

50. "Being there" is used in the same way as the Sartrean expression *être-là*. The monumentality described here is close to the one found in the Rossian discourse on the architecture of cities; it refers to the standing of "primary elements" (elementi primarii): cf. A. Rossi, *L'Architettura della Città* (Milano, 1973).

51. Eldem himself recognizes the importance of the vertical window in his work. In relating the latter to the different interpretations of Perret and Le Corbusier, he finds his approach closer to that of Le Corbusier. He argues, however, that traditional Turkish architecture reconciles the two differing solutions by having a horizontal procession of vertical windows: interview with Eldem, June 11, 1981.

52. Cf. Bektaş's answer to the questionnaire of *Mimarlık* 12 (December, 1970).

53. Cengiz Bektaş, "Proje ve Uygulama" (Project and Implementation) (Ankara, 1979), p. 58: also recognizes this holistic symbolism.

54. The usage of "scale" here is close to Boudon's polysemic use of the term: P. Boudon, *Sur l'espace architectural* (Paris, 1971), pp. 51-70.

55. It is worth quoting the passage at length in Zevi's eloquent Italian style: "Saturi di technologia e di obiettivismo razionale ... gli architetti si sono rivolti di nuovo alla tradizione, hanno discetatto di preesistenza ambientali, hanno esemplato i loro edifici su prototipi antichi, ma con disarmante superficialità.... Questo è il prezzo che la generazione di mezzo paga per aver abbraciato l'ideologia antistorica dei maestri senza discutarla, e poi per averla, d'un tratto, rifiutata senza vera elaborazione." B. Zevi, "Il Futuro del Passato in Architettura," *l'Architettura* 9 (no. 98, 1963), pp. 578-579.

56. It is worth mentioning the work of two contemporary Turkish poets with regard to the revival of historical connotations: Turgut Uyar used the title *Divan* (1971) for one of his collections, which Ece Ayhan semi-implicitly but severely criticized in his *Ortodoksluklar* (Orthodoxies, 1972). But these later "orthodoxies" are largely inspired in style and imagery by the complex heritage of the cosmopolitan Istanbul folk culture. [*Divan* means a collection of classical Ottoman poetry.]

57. See Cansever, *Thoughts and Architecture*.

58. This building won a prize in the 1980 Aga Khan Awards for Architecture. The event led to a lively discussion on nationalism, historicity, regionalism, and Islamism in the Turkish architectural milieu: see D. Kuban in *Milliyet Sanat Dergisi* 12 (15 November 1980); A. Yücel in *Çevre* 9-10 (1980); B. Güvenç in *Mimarlık* 3 (March, 1981); A. Arel in *Mimarlık* 4 (April, 1981); A. Yücel in *Mimarlık* 5 (May, 1981); R. Holod with D. Rastorfer, eds., *Architecture and Community: Building in the Islamic World Today* (New York, 1983).

59. J.P. Bonta, *Architecture and its Interpretations* (London, 1980), p. 29.

60. See U. Eco, *Le Forme del Contenuto* (Milano, 1971), Part I.

61. See J. Mukařovský, "On the Problem of Functions in Architecture," in J. Burbank and P. Steiner, eds., *Form, Sign and Function: Selected Writings of Jan Mukařovský* (New Haven, 1982); *idem*, "Sul problema delle funzioni nell'architettura," in *Il Significato dell'Estetica* (Torino, 1973), pp. 366-381.

62. The contemporary works of J. Castex and P. Panerai shed light on the generative typology of the eighteenth century French theoretician C.N. Durand: cf. P. Panerai, "Typologies," A. Yücel, tr., "Beaubourg, Tipin Ölümü ya da Dirilişi," *Çevre* 3 (1980).

63. The term "co-reality" is the English equivalent of *correaltà*, which is used by Tafuri for Max Bense's concept of *Mitwirklichkeit*. For his argument, see M. Tafuri, *Progetto e Utopia*, p. 144. However, it should be noted that Tafuri uses the term in a socially aware context as opposed to Bense's purely aesthetic concept. The usage here is closer to that of Tafuri.

CHAPTER VIII

TO HOUSE
THE NEW CITIZENS:
HOUSING POLICIES
AND MASS HOUSING

Yıldız Sey

Turkey's population is now approaching sixty million. Due to the high rate of population growth and insufficient facilities, the country is faced with a severe housing shortage. It is difficult to meet the annual demands, estimated at 350,000 units, because of limited financial resources. This chapter aims to review briefly the housing policies and mass housing production in Turkey since 1923. A chronological approach is preferred, focusing on the achievements during the Republican period rather than listing shortcomings in housing policies and mass housing production due to economic constraints. The critical examination of the Turkish experience, it is hoped, will be instructive for the problem of housing in developing countries. After a brief reference to the Ottoman background, housing policies and the implementation of mass housing schemes will be presented in four periods defined by particular political and economic trends: 1923-1933, 1933-1946, 1946-1960, and post-1960.

The political and economic collapse of the Ottoman Empire had not allowed for a comprehensive housing strategy in its final decades. Inadequate documentation limits our ability to ascertain whether there had even been the notion of a housing policy within Ottoman administration. However, the Ottoman state did have a long tradition of settlement policies which could be considered as a precedent. The state's intervention in population distribution in order to achieve its economic aims constituted the basis of this tradition. According to Erder, a settlement policy as a part of economic planning was a method borrowed from the Byzantine state.[1] It is known, for example, that houses and credit were made available in order to revive the economies of newly conquered towns which had been depopulated. The programs of the state included mass resettlement to replace populations who had fled.[2] Unfortunately, we do not have any documentation of the actual building activity in such cases. Neither do we know whether there existed a coordinated building implementation program in the modern sense. On the other hand, as a result of the accelerated refugee movement during the collapse of the

Empire, at least 1,000,000 people were resettled in Anatolia. This pattern continued between 1912 and 1915 when 250,000 people were resettled, and after 1920,when 400,000 were resettled.[3] Since it is evident that an adequate number of dwellings could not have been built by the state, it can be deduced that building activities were carried out by individuals receiving credits and land.

Organized residential development for certain client groups began in major metropolitan areas, especially Istanbul, during the second half of the nineteenth century. These housing clusters, built under the influence of Western models, are the only extant examples of multi-unit dwellings from the Ottoman period. These small-scale clusters were built for "Muslim and non-Muslim small merchants, tradesmen, artisans and petty bureaucrats,"

Fig. 139 Balyan and Balyan, Townhouses (Akaretler), Beşiktaş, Istanbul, 1870.

[4] and they differed greatly from the traditional Istanbul houses. Among the most interesting examples are Beşiktaş Akaretler (Fig. 139), built for palace personnel by Abdülaziz, and Taksim Surp Agop houses (1890).

The most significant low-income housing project of the Ottoman period was undertaken only a few years before the proclamation of the Republic. In the wake of the infamous Istanbul fire of 1918, in which 7,500 houses were destroyed, a complex of 124 houses and twenty-five shops was built on a site belonging to the Ministry of Pious Foundations, financed through private donations.[5] This complex, consisting of four blocks, is also one of Kemalettin Bey's most important works attributed to the First National Architectural Movement (Figs. 26-28, 140).[6]

Fig. 140 Kemalettin Bey, Harikzedegân (Fire Victims) Apartments, Istanbul, 1921.

The limited resources of the new Republic were allocated to other sectors and little was done for housing during the first years of the Republic. The government was faced with the task of rebuilding the devastations of the war; in addition, refugees coming from the former provinces had to be resettled in Anatolia. Yet, establishment of the new capital necessitated the building of housing for governmental personnel. In conformity with the economic policies formulated in 1923, the private sector was encouraged to participate in the rebuilding of cities as well as in providing housing for the exchanged population.[7] These economic policies included incentives for domestic and foreign construction companies to assure increased private-sector participation. Among these incentives were tax relief for new housing and exemption from custom duties for imported building materials. To coordinate these activities, the Ministry of Exchange and Settlement was established. Despite these measures, the anticipated results could not be obtained. Refugees were obliged to settle in substandard and unsanitary housing.[8]

The lack of both capital and construction materials exacerbated this situation. The building materials industry that was begun in the Ottoman period was not capable of providing for large-scale construction activity. The capacity of the cement industry, inaugurated with the establishment of the Darıca factory in 1910, had reached only 40,000 tons per year.[9] The first foundry to produce construction iron was established in Istanbul in 1926.[10] In addition, there were very few construction firms capable of undertaking large-scale projects, and the industry as a whole suffered from shortages of architects, engineers and other technical personnel.

Shortages notwithstanding, the building of the new capital, both its administrative and residential districts, proceeded apace according to a master plan. Apart from a plan contemplated for a limited section of Izmir, this was the first comprehensive city planning effort in Turkey. In 1924, Heussler prepared two plans for the two sections of Ankara, the old city and Yenişehir.[11] Shortly thereafter, a 198-unit residential project for government officials was begun. However, due to land speculation, costs escalated well beyond the initial estimates with the result that this district intended for lower-income groups became an area where high-income groups built luxurious houses and apartments. Civil servants, meanwhile, continued to live in difficult conditions in old Ankara houses. This situation is described in Atay's *Çankaya*:

> When we bought large tracts of land in the vicinity of Yenişehir to turn over to the Municipality, we had neglected to include a certain article in the law; that plots not exceeding in size required for a single building be sold only to those who would build on them during the year of purchase.[12]

Lack of experience in planning caused the development to move in directions quite different from those the officials had intended. In this case, a project begun with the best of intentions was subverted by the profit motive.

In 1924 the Municipal Law of Ankara and the Law of Eminent Domain which would facilitate the provision of public lands for the building of the capital was prepared. While such legislation was being prepared, the acute demand for housing continued. In a few cases, buildings were constructed without permit on other people's property. The same year, the first law that called for the demolition of such illegally constructed buildings was enacted. Finally, there was a concerted attempt to prevent such problems. In 1928, the Directorate of Reconstruction was established and a law was promulgated to require all construction to be approved by this agency. Hermann Jansen's plan for Ankara was also completed in the same year.

The notion of city planning in the modern sense had arrived in Turkey. While the plan was being implemented, new approaches were being taken to solve the persisting problem of housing low-income civil servants. In 1926, Emlâk ve Eytam Bankası, today's Emlâk Kredi Bankası, (Real Estate and Credit Bank) was founded. To provide credit for new construction, a special law authorizing the Ministry of Treasury to use treasury funds for building government housing was promulgated and Imar Bankası (Reconstruction Bank) was founded.[13] Yet, the housing needs of the civil servants could not be answered in the short term; thus another law, promulgated in 1929, called for providing rent subsidies to civil servants in Ankara. In this period, the Directorate of Pious Foundations began renting subsidized flats, and some banks and public sector companies built residences for their staff. The civil servant housing projects designed by Arif Hikmet Koyunoğlu and Kemalettin Bey, the First and Second Vakıf Apartments (Figs. 37, 38, 141) in Ankara by Kemalettin Bey, and the staff residences of the Agricultural Bank are the best examples of multi-unit housing of the First National Architectural Movement.[14]

Fig. 141 Kemalettin Bey, Second Vakıf Apartments, Ankara, 1928.

Between 1928 and 1930 certain codes pertaining to city planning were introduced through legislation to facilitate the construction of housing. Most prominent were laws governing construction and land use in Ankara. The new municipal law took into account the problem of low-income housing, and the Public Health Law introduced minimum standards for residential buildings.[15] However, the Depression soon began to affect Turkey and construction activity slowed down appreciably. The program of the fifth Inönü government (1931) called for "precautionary measures in government spending" and yet hoped "to begin new reconstruction programs without causing repercussions in the economic and fiscal order."[16]

The housing situation in other cities was not much different. Available housing vacated during the exchange of populations was in poor condition and could not be renovated because of the lack of funds. This inadequacy was further compounded by the influx of some 500,000 migrants from Bulgaria and Yugoslavia between 1923 and 1929, who could only be given limited subventions.[17] Thus, the first decade of the Republic is marked on the one hand by the formulation of necessary legislation for the long term and by stop-gap measures for the immediate problem.

Although the first Five-Year Plan (1933) did not include housing, it led to a revitalization of the construction industry because of the industrial investments that it required. The notion of "low-cost housing" was introduced into architectural terminology. Rational-functional trends[18] adopted by young architects under the influence of contemporary architectural movements in Europe also figured in the search for new low-cost housing types.[19] The low-cost rowhouse project planned by Seyfettin Nasih [Arkan] for Ankara is a typical example of such trends (Fig. 142).[20]

Like most of his colleagues, Nasih followed the masters of the Bauhaus

Fig. 142 Seyfettin Nasih [Arkan], Low-cost Row House Project, Ankara, 1933.

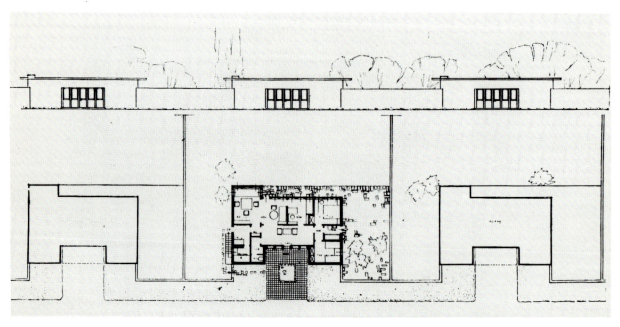

and emphasized the economy of mass production. Yet, while these efforts remained in project stage, construction of multi-storey apartment complexes was being undertaken at an accelerated pace. The development of such complexes for high-income bureaucrats, merchants and industrialists was not paralleled by building for low-income groups, The resulting imbalance was described by Martin Wagner, a consultant to the Municipality of Istanbul: "The new residential buildings constructed in Turkish cities are not intended for the needy, which constitute eighty percent of the population, but for the wealthy six percent."[21]

The construction of low-cost housing was further constrained by several factors. As a result of land speculation, real estate values increased sharply. This was also paralleled by increases in the cost of basic construction materials, especially that of cement. The price of cement was consistently set at a level twice or three times higher than the prevailing rates in Europe by a cartel established by foreign capital which controlled the industry. The state attempted to introduce corrective measures such as price controls and even nationalization of the industry in 1938.[22] However, in view of the large demand versus the limited production, these attempts failed. A similar situation prevailed in the rental market. Although a rent control law was promulgated, rents nevertheless kept increasing because of the inadequate supply of residential units. This situation paved the way for

Fig. 143   Burhan Arif, A Village Project, 1935.

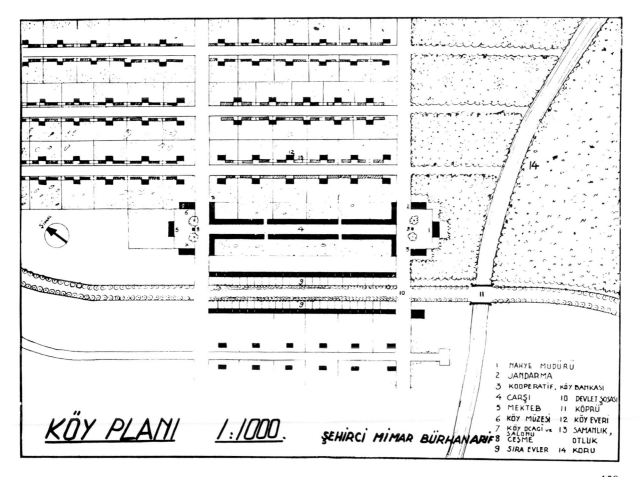

KÖY PLANI   1:1000.   ŞEHIRCI MIMAR BÜRHAN ARIF

1 NAHYE MÜDÜRÜ
2 JANDARMA
3 KOOPERATIF, KÖY BANKASI
4 ÇARŞI   10 DEVLET ŞOSASI
5 MEKTEB   11 KÖPRÜ
6 KÖY MÜZESI   12 KÖY EVERI
7 KÖY OCAGI ve   13 SAMANLIK,
   SALONU   OTLUK
8 ÇESME
9 SIRA EVLER   14 KORU

the establishment of building cooperatives. The first of these was Bahçelievler Yapı Kooperatifi (1935) in Ankara. Housing for workers and peasants became a major concern of the state in the 1930s. The program of the 1937 Bayar government included provisions for housing built by municipalities. Factories to produce basic building materials such as iron, steel and cement also began to be erected.

In order to promote modernity in rural areas, four new villages were constructed (Fig. 143). As explained in a contemporary source, mistakes plagued these projects due to a shortage of skilled labor and an unfamiliarity with the needs of villages and villagers. In many respects the buildings were implemented as if they had been in urban areas.[23] In order to avoid repetition of such mistakes a competition for a prototype village-house was held. The comprehensive report prepared for this competition exemplifies the official view regarding village housing and settlement. This report decries the waste of resources caused by inadequate preliminary studies. It then proposes the following approach:

> Expenditure of public funds to provide housing for the villager but using material unfamiliar to him would turn the peasant into a parasite. For no young peasant is capable of spending such amounts of money for housing. And, therefore, he would expect the state to build him a house, just like the one the state had built for his father; if this is not done, he would think that the state is in a decline, a reversal due to the neglect of the peasant. Hence, he will become an enemy of the regime.

This document clearly indicates that village housing was conceived as a means of strengthening the Republican regime. The same author expounds the ideological basis of village planning during that period:

> The village project must be prepared by a son of the Republic who knows the village, ideals of this regime, and Turkish culture with which the Turkish villager must be inculcated. In the place of the mosque, there ought to be a coffeehouse built in the center of the village. In this coffeehouse must be a radio provided by state funds, a stage to accommodate itinerant theatrical performances and film shows for propaganda purposes, and a reading area which would contain books and newspapers sent there by the state.

Thus, on the one hand a new village design was to provide an appropriate environment for the dissemination of the official ideology. On the other, the necessity to consider the basic culture and traditions of the villagers was also stressed: "Before designing the new village house, it is necessary to study the house that the villager builds for himself."[24] To which extent these views were incorporated in the prize-winning projects is a moot point.[25] Moreover, there is no detailed information in the implementation of these projects. Nevertheless, there have been various projects designed and implemented, which reflected the aforementioned approach such as those of Burhan Arif and Behçet Ünsal.[26]

The workers' quarters built for Kömür-İş coal workers in Zonguldak and for the employees of KIAŞ coalworks in Kozlu constitute the first significant examples of workers' residences (Figs. 144, 145). In explaining his work, Seyfettin Arkan, the architect of both projects, pointed out how he was striving to achieve the goals of the Republican revolution through the use of science and technology, a widespread attitude in architectural circles at the time.[27] Although he claimed that traditional values were taken into consideration, both projects are chiefly influenced by the dominant architectural trends of Europe.

Just as housing construction began to be an important issue for the state during the 1930s, so too architects began to develop new approaches. The manifestation of the Kemalist principles of populism in architecture can be observed in housing. Ünsal, who claimed the economic and rational approach in housing to be the spirit of the time, reflected the prevailing opinion of the younger architects:

> The dominant characteristic of the new architecture lies in its popular approach. The old architecture started with temple, palace, and castle and then grew. The subject matter of the new architecture is the house.... The purpose of today's architecture is neither to erect temples to serve the religion, nor to build palaces to please the king, but to utilize architecture to solve the problems of the peasant, worker and the people who are living in unhealthy and substandard conditions.[28]

The importance attached by the regime to housing and settlement is reflected in Atatürk's speech in the National Assembly on October 1, 1933. He stressed the significance of city planning in the cultural development of the nation and proposed a center to undertake city planning for the whole country.[29] The hiring of foreign architects and city planners, beginning in the late 1920s, is another indication of these priorities. While these foreign experts positively affected the development of Turkish cities (by introducing contemporary approaches), their imposition of alien urban forms had a negative effect on the shape and texture of life. The city planning of Jansen and Wagner introduced the new city planning of Europe. Wagner's warnings concerning the possible negative consequences of liberalism in the development of cities and his writings on the significance of culture and tradition in city planning are noteworthy. However, the forms and materials proposed in his low-cost post-disaster housing project prepared in the wake of the 1939 Erzincan earthquake are a revealing example of how little he knew about the Anatolian village and peasant. His single-room prefabricated units, designed to be built of enameled steel, fiberglass and copper, materials very expensive and difficult to obtain in Turkey, were also unusual in appearance. The following description of the heating and cooling systems shows why reliance on foreign experts was met with great skepticism in Turkey: "In these low-cost houses, electricity would be used not only for cooking, but also for lighting and heating. Electrical systems will be placed in a dome-like form under the roof along with the ventilation system."[30] An article by Janet Jones about this project in *The New York Times* can be read as an example of black humor:

> In his plans for the low-cost housing for the poor, Professor Wagner imitated nature and especially shelters

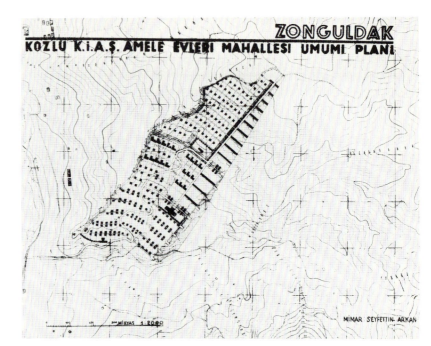

Fig. 144 Arkan, Kömür-İş Workers' Housing, Kozlu, Zonguldak, 1935. General plan.

Fig. 145 Arkan, Kömür-İş Workers' Housing, Kozlu, Zonguldak, 1935. Model.

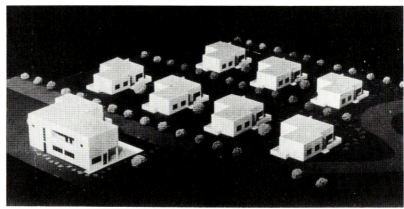

used by primitive men and animals. Having painted these houses blue, yellow, red and white in his drawings, the professor has given them an appearance of a flower bed.[31]

No sooner had the implementation of the policies of the 1930s begun than the country plunged into a new period of recession due to World War II. Although Turkey did not enter the war, it was nevertheless affected by it and housing construction declined appreciably after 1939.[32] At that time there were frequent complaints in the press that, although construction activity had increased since the founding of the Republic, this activity had not been developed in a planned and systematic way; that in spite of some legal measures, planning for reconstruction had been delayed;[33] that since housing was a social matter, it ought to have been regulated by the state;[34] and that because the state had not adequately planned the production of construction materials, prices increased without state control.[35]

Ankara was again one of the cities in which this crisis was most acutely felt. The population there increased at a rate well above estimates and overdensification became a major problem. Difficulties were encountered in starting houses planned by the newly established cooperatives, in the completion of construction underway, and in obtaining land and material. The high interest rates of government loans were an additional burden. Professional societies searched for solutions to the problem of housing production. The Turkish Economic Society in collaboration with the Turkish Architects' Association, the Engineers' Association and the Turkish Law Society established a commission in order to identify the measures to be taken to alleviate this crisis. This commission, which also included Professor Ernst Reuter, presented the following recommendations:

—putting a stop to all activities that would result in a reduction of housing available;

—encouraging the conversion into housing of all covered spaces;

—erecting temporary shelters on vacant lots;

—constructing mudbrick houses and barracks for poor people in urban fringe areas;

—applying rent control to new buildings;

—encouraging multiple tenancy;

—levying luxury tax on people living in large houses;

—limiting rental rights of furnished units;

—controlling rents of furnished units;

—making better use of the residential buildings occupied by government offices;

—founding municipal housing offices;

—distributing housing according to a waiting list.

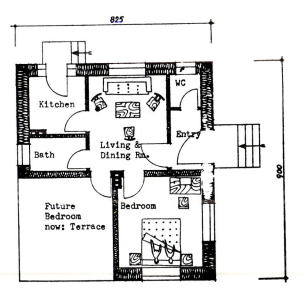

Fig. 146 Sümerbank (State Textile Industries) Workers' Housing, Kayseri, 1943. Site plan and prototype.

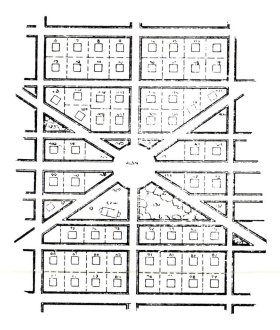

These measures, unfortunately, were not incorporated into the policies of public institutions.

The question of workers' housing was also a serious concern for the state in the 1930s. First to be funded were residences for the employees of the newly established Sümerbank (state textile industries). Although this initiative fell short of providing adequate housing, it was nevertheless a significant undertaking. Other such examples were the workers' housing at the Nazilli, Ereğli, Kayseri (Fig. 146), Hereke textile factories and the Izmir paper plant.[36]

Kessler at the Faculty of Economics of the University of Istanbul and Reuter, a city planner at the Political Science School, greatly contributed to the research on housing. Their work on cooperatives, and policies and financing of housing, led to a greater awareness of these issues.

Meanwhile, the problem of low-income civil servant housing had not yet been solved, and, until the end of World War II, legislative solutions continued to be explored. For example, in 1944, the Law of Civil Servant Housing was promulgated. According to this law, which gave priority to those living in Ankara, civil servants and military personnel who did not own a house would be provided with residential units in buildings to be constructed for this purpose.[37]

The most important project under this law was the 434-unit Saraçoğlu Quarter in Ankara (Fig. 147). It was designed by Bonatz, begun in 1944 and completed in 1947. Likewise, 275 residential units for civil servants were constructed in some eastern provinces. However, all were criticized for not being adequate.[38] While there was no appreciable increase in the production of housing, the decade prior to 1946 marked the beginning of concerted conceptual development.

Because of the rapid and unplanned urbanization after World War II,

Fig. 147 Bonatz, Saraçoğlu Quarter, Ankara, 1944. Site plan.

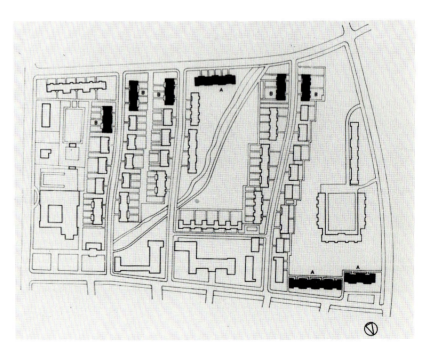

especially in the 1950s, discussed by Tekeli and Tapan earlier in this book, the housing shortage reached critical proportions. The aggregate growth in urban population, which had been 20.1 percent between 1940 and 1950, jumped to 80.2 percent in the next decade.[39] As a result of migrations from rural to urban areas, especially to Ankara, Istanbul and Izmir, demand for housing much exceeded the supply. The rise in rents and real estate prices led to the formation of fringe settlements, the so-called gecekondus. The number of gecekondu units, estimated at 25,000 in 1948, reached 80,000 in

Fig. 148 Aru and Gorbon, First Levent District, Istanbul, 1947-1951. Site plan.

Fig. 149 Aru and Gorbon, First Levent District, Istanbul, 1947-1951. Single units.

Fig. 150 Özden and Turgut, Koşuyolu District, Istanbul, 1951. Site plan.

Fig. 151 Özden and Turgut, Koşuyolu District, Istanbul, 1951. General view of row houses.

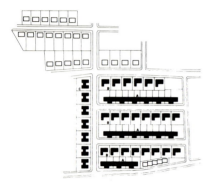

Fig. 152 Project Office of the Emlâk Kredi Bankası, 82-unit District, Diyarbakır, 1954. Site plan.

Fig. 153 Aru, Fourth Levent District, Istanbul, 1956. Site plan.

Fig. 154 Aru, Fourth Levent District, Istanbul, 1956. General view.

1953 and 240,000 in 1960.[40] Measures to prevent gecekondu construction and to demolish those constructed were taken. The people continued to improvise their own solutions where government could not respond.

In this inflationary era of rapid economic growth, certain commercial groups acquired new wealth. The luxurious residences built in the cities by the newly acquired money stood in stark contrast to the peripheral gecekondu settlements. This contrast was noted by Kessler: "The differences between the housing conditions of the rich upper classes and those of the poor masses in today's Istanbul are greater than those observed in almost all European metropolises. Such luxury is to be seen neither in London nor Paris, neither in Amsterdam nor in Milan." [41]

Some corrective measures were undertaken, however. First among them was the law establishing the Emlâk Kredi Bankası. The aims of this bank included providing long-term low-interest credit, engaging in industrial and commercial production of housing and construction materials, and building and selling residential units.[42] The Levent district in Istanbul, begun in 1947, is one of the first developments of this bank (Figs. 148, 149). The 391-unit Levent project was followed by the 413-unit Koşuyolu district in Istanbul (Figs. 150, 151), begun in 1951, and an 82-unit district in Diyarbakır, begun in 1954 (Fig. 152). These projects, consisting of single- or two-storey individual or row-houses with gardens, were designed for middle-income families. With the exception of the Koşuyolu project, these units were too spacious—some of them were as large as 180 square meters—to be considered subsidized housing.

The second important legislation of the period was the Building Encouragement Act. This law, which required that vacant plots be turned over to municipalities, and that municipalities in turn distribute these to homeless people, also included measures to lower the costs of transportation and import of building materials. Despite their intent, these measures failed and low-income groups did not find relief. Gecekondu

construction continued to spread while multi-storey dwellings were being built at a rapid rate for the needs of middle-income groups. In 1958, the earlier Directorate was reorganized as the Ministry of Reconstruction and Settlement to regulate and organize all activities pertaining to housing.

The end of the 1950s saw expanded activity in house construction undertaken by the Emlâk Kredi Bankası. The new projects called for multiple-storey residences instead of single units surrounded by gardens. The first implementation of this type was the 345-unit Fourth Levent District consisting of single houses, row houses and highrise blocks (Figs. 153, 154). The construction of this quarter began in 1956 and was completed in 1960. This quarter, which has a low population density of 102 persons per hectare, includes public facilities such as movie theaters and sport facilities. Beginning in 1957, the same bank started building on Atatürk Bulvarı, one of the denser sections of the city (Figs. 155, 156). Both of these housing complexes reflected the characteristics of the International Style which was prevalent in Turkey, but they were not in conformity with the bank's aims. The periodical *Arkitekt* describes this conflict:

> The apartments were designed too spaciously. The approach to the housing problem is still fraught with unfortunate misconceptions and misdirections on the part of the Municipality of Istanbul and of the Emlâk Kredi Bankası. The task of the municipality is not to build spacious residences but to provide small and cheap rental units of 2-3 rooms.[43]

Other authors also criticized the policies of the bank.[44]

The bank's most comprehensive project has been the Ataköy complex (Istanbul) which was designed as a brand new city for 50,000 people (Figs. 102, 157). This project began in 1957 and is still in progress. The first neighborhood consisting of 618 units was completed in 1961 and also included a wide range of public facilities. The above-mentioned criticism has also been leveled against Ataköy. Costs have reached levels affordable only by upper-income groups. The bank has also been accused of being a leading contributor to land speculation because of its policies.

Massive foreign aid to Turkey began in the post-war years. Along with it came its own experts. Foreign architects and city planners had been employed earlier, when the profession in Turkey was still young and unspecialized. The situation in the 1950s was no longer the same, yet foreign experts were brought in to find solutions for such an important national problem as housing. First to arrive were experts from Skidmore, Owings and Merrill, who produced a report in 1951 on the reconstruction and housing problem. Then, several individuals and groups of experts came either by invitation of the government or of the United Nations. Among these experts who prepared reports on housing were Charles Abrams, Holmes Perkins, experts from the Productivity Agency of the OECD, Donald Manson, Bernard Wagner, the Housing Committee of the EEC, Frederic Bath, Chailloux-Dantel, E.H.B. Wedler.[45] While some reports contained in-depth analyses and pertinent observations, others were only sample solution packages not based on local research. Manson and Wagner dwelt especially on the problem of workers' housing. Since the

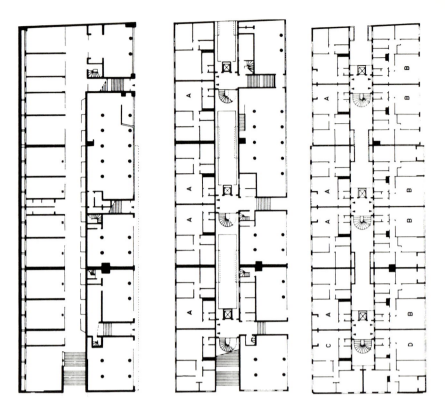

Fig. 155 Project Office of the Emlâk Kredi Bankası, Atatürk Bulvarı Apartments, Istanbul, 1957. Typical floor plans.

Fig. 156 Project Office of the Emlâk Kredi Bankası, Atatürk Bulvarı Apartments, Istanbul, 1957. General view.

founding of the Social Security Organization in 1946, legislation had been passed to provide credit for workers' housing. However, it was soon understood that credits made available to building cooperatives organized by social security beneficiaries could not solve the problem because low-income workers could not meet their high interest rates and repayment terms.

Fig. 157 Menteşe and Project Office of the Emlâk Kredı Bankası, Ataköy Development, Phase I, 1969. Site plan.

Disaster housing was another area of concern. Turkey is in a significant earthquake zone and therefore vulnerable. A law stipulating precautionary measures and guidelines for relief work was enacted in 1959. This law provided the general principles for rebuilding, whereas in the past a new law had to be enacted in the wake of each disaster.

Economic and political crises led to the May 27, 1960 coup. The military government took a different approach to the housing problem. The National Unity Committee program, announced on July 11, 1960, stressed that housing construction would be undertaken within the larger framework of development plans. The same program also called for low-cost sanitary housing, and direct credit to those in need of housing.[46] The notion of subsidized housing came to Turkey in this period. The İnönü government of 1961 also stressed housing in its program and announced that it would give priority to the needs of low-income families.[47]

The 1961 Constitution, which included specific articles pertaining to housing, called for the establishment of the State Planning Organization. Turkey entered a new period of planning in 1963. The four five-year development plans implemented after 1963 contained specific targets regarding housing. However, with the change of governments, modifications were made in these plans.

The first Five-Year Development Plan approached housing from the viewpoint of general economic and social development and aimed to achieve a reasonable balance between the housing need and resources.[48] It was proposed that investment for housing not exceed 20 percent of the overall investment. In order to satisfy the needs of as large a segment of people as possible, it called for realistic standards. As a result, a manual of standards for economical housing was prepared and legislation was enacted to provide tax relief only for housing conforming to these standards. The plan stated that unless alternative housing could be provided to gecekondu families, their houses were not to be demolished. The Gecekondu Law of 1966 proposed the preservation of the gecekondus that could be upgraded and the elimination of the ones that could not. A construction program was conceived to provide housing for gecekondu dwellers whose houses would be eliminated and for other low-income groups who could not afford alternate housing.

The Second Plan restricted government investment in housing to seventeen percent of total investments and defined the role of the state as that of a regulator rather than an investor. This plan fundamentally differed from the first because it called for the "solution of the housing problem within the framework of market mechanisms."[49]

In the Third Plan, which placed less emphasis on housing, investment was further restricted to 15.7 percent of the total. The most significant aspect of this plan in terms of housing was the encouragement of cooperatives and the support of entrepreneurs.

By the time the fourth Five-Year Plan was prepared, the annual demand for housing had reached 300,000 units. The Fourth Plan emphasized the need for a new technology and organizational means to increase building. It also proposed incentives for local governments to contribute to the housing solution. In practice, housing production between 1960 and 1981 did not fulfill the principles and targets set forth in the five-year plans.

The trend of building multi-storey apartment houses began in the 1950s and continued until the end of the 1960s. Throughout this period emphasis was on multi-unit single buildings. In the 1970s, however, the trend began to shift towards multi-block complexes which could be more accurately called mass housing (Fig. 158).[50] In the latter period, developments by Workers' Insurance Cooperatives played an important role, although they fell short of fulfilling the need. The activities of several other cooperatives supported by unions are noteworthy. Among the more successful projects were Merter Sitesi of Maden-İş and Aydınlıkevler Sitesi of Türk-İş. With some exceptions, these buildings have no significant architectural characteristics.

Fig. 158 ME-SA Group, Çankaya Development, Ankara, 1972-1976.

The credit facilities of Workers' Insurance created a demand in the housing market and provided a reliable pool of clients for contractors. Until the mid-1970s a great number of multi-storey complexes conforming to the credit requirements of Workers' Insurance were built. In addition, apartment complexes for high-income groups also began to be erected in more expensive sections of big cities. This production of high-cost dwellings, which obviously cannot be considered as mass housing, rose rapidly until 1979, when the economic crisis slowed it down. The Emlâk Kredi Bankası has continued to build apartments on a very limited scale in several cities, especially in Istanbul.

Another significant undertaking since the 1960s has aimed at providing housing for military personnel. During this period, 1,658 units have been built for the officers retired in 1960. OYAK (Saving and Investment Society for Military Personnel) emerged as one of the largest organizations supplying non-profit housing to its members.

Public funds have also been used to provide housing in gecekondu prevention areas and disaster areas. Implementation in both these areas has been plagued by problems. Low-income housing built in gecekondu prevention areas has serious shortcomings. Because of poor programming and planning both these and post-disaster houses fall short of answering needs.

Developments in housing technology, construction of vacation houses and resort complexes, and the role of municipalities are three significant issues that have emerged in the 1970s. The first mass housing project utilizing industrial technology was the complex for the workers of Ereğli Iron and Steel Works (Fig. 159). The design chosen at a competition in 1962 was implemented by employing heavy prefabricated panels. Prefabricated elements have been used in a few other projects also. Efforts to implement new technology have increased in recent years. The first

Fig. 159 Sanlı, Tuncer and Acar, Workers' Housing, Ereğli Iron and Steel Works, Zonguldak, 1962.

initiative towards achieving continuous production was taken by the Ministry of Reconstruction and Settlement in 1968. A plant capable of producing 500 prefabricated wooden housing units annually was followed in 1969 by the erection of another plant to provide concrete prefabricated elements. The plants were considered the only means to provide a sufficient number of post-disaster houses in a short time. Because of organizational problems, these plants have not been working efficiently (Figs. 160, 161).

There were also some attempts at prefabrication by the private sector. As a result, significant progress was made in the production of prefabricated small components for walls and floors. Although closed prefabricated systems were commonly being used in the construction of industrial buildings, industrialization of housing production was still at an experimental stage. Methods such as the utilization of a tubular framework to accelerate in-situ production were becoming widely used.

Fig. 160 KIGI, Post-disaster Housing, Bingöl, 1969. Prefabricated single-storey buildings.

Fig. 161 Ministry of Reconstruction and Settlement, Post-disaster Housing, Gediz.

Many buildings were constructed by this method in the late 1970s. The first plant to produce large prefabricated panels was erected in Manisa by Betonsan under the patent of the Mitscheck System of Austria. These panels were first used at Petkim Complex in Aliağa. Because of inadequate preparation, the outcome was not successful, and the plant has stopped its production for the time being. A second plant to produce heavy panels for housing production, after the Balancy System of France, has recently been completed in Istanbul.

The construction of vacation houses began in the 1960s and peaked in the following decade. The idea of a second house became a new trend in the holiday patterns of middle-income groups and was promoted energetically by contractors. The construction of resort houses rapidly increased in a haphazard fashion and resulted in the spoiling of the coastline in many places. Finally in 1978, a new law imposed limitations on the utilization of coastal sites. Various types of vacation complexes were built both by state organizations to provide resort facilities for their personnel, and by the private sector for commercial purposes, including rentals, term ownership and outright sale (Figs. 132-134, 162-164).

Fig. 162 Gürsel, Çubuk and Güner, Selimiye Holiday Village, Side, Antalya, 1978. Site plan. Original site chosen for this project was declared a conservation area and the present village was erected on a different site.

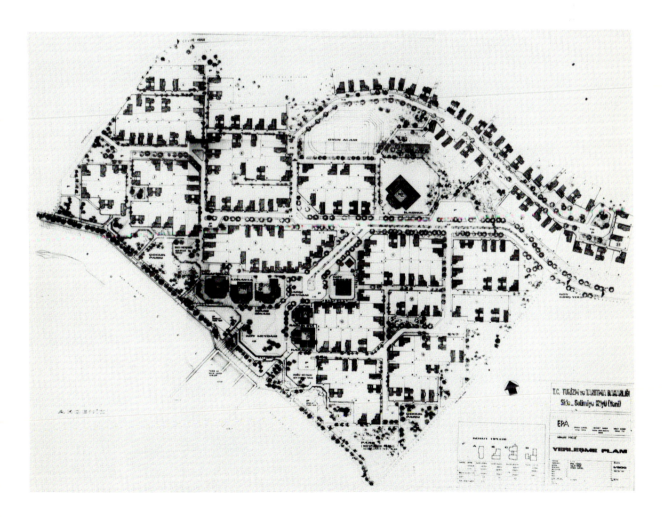

Fig. 164 Gürsel, Çubuk and Ertürün, Çapa Holiday Village, Bodrum, 1979. Detail of the village.

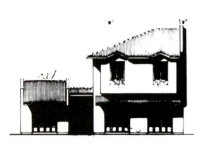

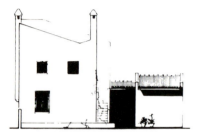

Fig. 163 Gürsel, Çubuk and Güner, Selimiye Holiday Village, Side, Antalya, 1978. Front and side elevation of a single unit.

In the laws of the early Republic, individual municipalities had been given specific responsibilities over infrastructure and building codes, but they did not assume a significant role in housing until the 1970s. Over the last decade several municipalities have undertaken experimental programs to alleviate the still existing bottleneck in housing. The most comprehensive programs were begun in Ankara and in Izmit, projects of 50,000 and 30,000 units respectively.[51] The smaller-scale projects of Cumhuriyet Quarter in Edirne (Fig. 165, 166) and municipal housing in Çorum (Fig. 167) consisting of 1,000 houses each are also worth mentioning. Some of these programs have not yet been implemented. Although these projects are not without problems, they nevertheless constitute a significant alternative.

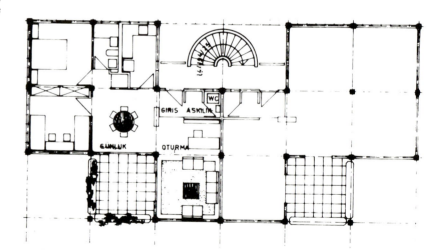

Fig. 165 Bektaş', Cumhuriyet District, Edirne, 1975. Sample apartment plan.

Fig. 166 Bektaş, Cumhuriyet District, Edirne, 1975. Elevation.

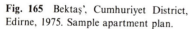

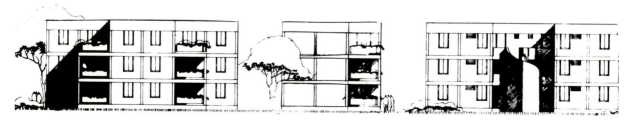

Today Turkish society still faces a vast and complex problem of housing. A recent law has provided means for encouraging both the users and builders to utilize new technologies for housing. However, it is too early to tell what the results will be, since this legislation primarily aims at creating financial resources and therefore would chiefly help upper-income groups.

Fig. 167 Çinici and Çinici, Bin Evler District, Çorum, 1973.

NOTES

1. L. Erder, "Türkiye'de Uygulanan Yerleşme Politikaları" (Settlement Policies in Turkey), in *İç Göçler* (Internal Migrations) (Ankara, 1970), p. 46.

2. *Ibid.*, p. 47.

3. *Ibid.*, p. 48.

4. A. Batur, N. Fersan and A. Yücel, "Istanbul'da Ondokuzuncu Yüzyıl Sıra Evleri" (Nineteenth Century Rowhouses in Istanbul) *ODTÜ Mimarlık Fakültesi Dergisi* (Journal of the Faculty of Architecture, METU) 5 (no. 2, 1979), pp. 185-205.

5. Y. Yavuz, *Mimar Kemalettin ve Birinci Ulusal Mimarlık Dönemi* (Mimar Kemalettin and the First National Architectural Period) (Ankara, 1981), p. 272.

6. Y. Yavuz, "Türkiye'de Çok Katlı Sosyal Konuta Ilk Örnek: Istanbul Lâleli'de Harikzedegân Katevleri" (The First Example of Subsidized Housing in Turkey: the Harikzedegân Apartments) *Çevre* 4 (1979), pp. 80-84.

7. I. Arar, *Hükümet Programları* (Government Programs) (Istanbul, 1968), pp. 34-35: The Program of the Fethi Okyar Cabinet, 5 September 1923.

8. *Ibid.*, p. 44: The Program of the Second Fethi Okyar Government, 27 November 1924.

9. D. Avcıoğlu, *Türkiye'nin Düzeni* (The Structure of Turkey) (Istanbul, 1968), p. 190.

10. *Ibid.*, p. 233.

11. Ü. Alsaç, *Türkiye'deki Mimarlık Düşüncesinin Cumhuriyet Dönemindeki Evrimi* (Development of Architectural Thought in Turkey During the Republican Period) (Trabzon, 1976), p. 230.

12. F.R. Atay, *Çankaya* (Istanbul, 1969), pp. 420-421.

13. Alsaç, *Türkiye'deki Mimarlık Düşüncesi*, p. 234.

14. I. Aslanoğlu, *1923-1938 Erken Cumhuriyet Dönemi Mimarlığı* (1923-1928 Architecture of the Early Republican Period) (Ankara, 1980), pp. 22-23.

15. Y. Sey, "Yapı Üretim Analizinde Sistem Yaklaşımı" (A Systems Approach to the Analysis of Building Production), mimeograph, Istanbul Technical University, 1971.

16. Arar, *Hükümet Programları*, p. 61.

17. V. Inkaya, "Türkiye'de Cumhuriyet Devrimi Başından Günümüze Kadar Konut Sorunu" (Housing Problem in Turkey Since the Republican Revolution) *Mimarlık* 107 (September, 1972), pp. 50-65.

18. Alsaç, *Türkiye'deki Mimarlık Düşüncesi*, p. 22.

19. S. Nasih, "Ankara Için Ucuz Aile Evi Tipleri" (Economical Family-House Types for Ankara) *Arkitekt* 5 (May, 1933), p. 174.

20. S. Nasih, "Ankara'da Sıra Evler Tipi: 2" (Row house Type for Ankara: 2) *Arkitekt* 12 (December, 1933), p. 382.

21. M. Wagner, "Türk Şehirleri ve Mevcut Sahalardan Istifade Ekonomisi" (Turkish Cities and the Economies of Utilizing Existing Spaces) *Arkitekt* 3 (March, 1938), p. 83.

22. Avcıoğlu, *Türkiye'nin Düzeni*, pp. 190-191.

23. A.Z. Kozanoğlu, "Köy Evleri Proje ve Yapıları Için Toplu Rapor" (Consolidated Report on the Design and Building of Village Houses) *Arkitekt* 7-8 (July-August, 1935), pp. 203-204.

24. *Ibid.*

25. Anon., "Köy Evleri Proje Müsabakası" (Village-House Project Competition) *Arkitekt* 3 (March, 1935), p. 93.

26. A. Mortaş, "Köy Projesi" (Village Project) *Arkitekt* 11-12 (November-December, 1935), p. 320.

27. S. Arkan, "Amele Evleri, Ilkokul, Mutfak, Çamaşılık Binası—Kozlu, Zonguldak" (Workers' Houses, Primary School, Kitchen, Laundry—Kozlu, Zonguldak) *Arkitekt* 9 (September, 1935), pp. 253-258.

28. B. Ünsal, "Ar ve Memleket Mimarlığının Kronolojisi Üzerine Düşünceler" (On Art and the Chronology of the Country's Architecture) *Arkitekt* 6 (June, 1935), pp. 182-186.

29. M. Wagner, "Inşa Etmeyen Bir Millet Yaşamıyor Demektir" (A Nation Which Does Not Build Does Not Live) *Arkitekt* 10-11 (October-November, 1937), pp. 276-278.

30. M. Wagner, "Zelzele Mıntıkası Için Düşünülmüş Mukavim, Standart Ev Projeleri" (Designs for Standard, Durable Houses in Earthquake Areas) *Arkitekt* 6 (June, 1940).

31. Quoted in *ibid.* Wagner does not cite *The New York Times* issue in which Janet Jones' article appeared.

32. Z. Sayar, "Imar Politikamızı Kuralım ve Teşkilâtlandıralım" (Let Us Establish and Organize Our Reconstruction Policies) *Arkitekt* 11-12 (1941-1942), p. 239.

33. Z. Sayar, "Bir Yapı ve Imar Politikamız Var mıdır?" (Do We Have a Building and Reconstruction Policy?) *Arkitekt* 5-6 (May-June, 1943), pp. 97-98.

34. E. Reuter, "Mesken Meselesinin Halli Çareleri" (Solutions for the Housing Problem) *Arkitekt* 9-10 (September-October, 1943), pp. 263-271.

35. Z. Sayar, "Yapı Işlerimizin Bugünkü Durumu" (The Present Situation in Building) *Arkitekt* 7-8 (July-August, 1943), pp. 143-144.

36. Anon., "Sümerbank Amele Evleri ve Mahalleleri" (Sümerbank Workers' Houses and Quarters) *Arkitekt* nos. 145-146 (1944), pp. 9-13.

37. R. Keleş, "Konut Sorunları ve Politikası" (Housing Problems and Policies) *Şehircilik* (City Planning) (Ankara, 1978), p. 615.

38. Z. Sayar, "Mesken Davası" (Housing Problem) *Arkitekt* nos. 171-172 (1946), pp. 49-50.

39. Keleş, *Şehircilik*, p. 26.

40. *Ibid.*, p. 660.

41. G. Kessler, "Istanbul'da Mesken Darlığı, Mesken Sefaleti, Mesken Inşaatı" (Housing Shortage, Housing Misery, Housing Construction in Istanbul) *Arkitekt* nos. 209-210 (1949), pp. 131-134.

42. Keleş, *Şehircilik*, p. 619.

43. Anon., "Istanbul Belediyesi, Türkiye Emlâk Kredi Bankası Blok Apartmanları Atatürk Bulvarı" (Municipality of Istanbul and Emlâk Kredi Bankası Multi-Storey Apartments Atatürk Bulvarı) *Arkitekt* no. 286 (1957), pp. 12-16.

44. Keleş, *Şehircilik*, p. 620.

45. *Ibid.*, 699-707.

46. Arar, *Hükümet Programları*, p. 322.

47. *Ibid.*, p. 335.

48. Keleş, *Şehircilik*, p. 635.

49. *Ibid.*, p. 639.

50. I. Tekeli, "Türkiye Kentlerinde Apartmanlaşma Sürecinde Iki Aşama" (Two Phases in the Apartment Building Process in Turkish Cities) *Çevre* 4 (1979), p. 79.

51. A. Bulca, T. Çavdar, I. Tekeli, E. Onaran, and A. Yücel, "Izmit Deneyinin Ardından" (After the Izmit Experiment) *Çevre* 4 (1979), pp. 53-59.

HERMANN JANSEN'S PLAN
FOR ANKARA

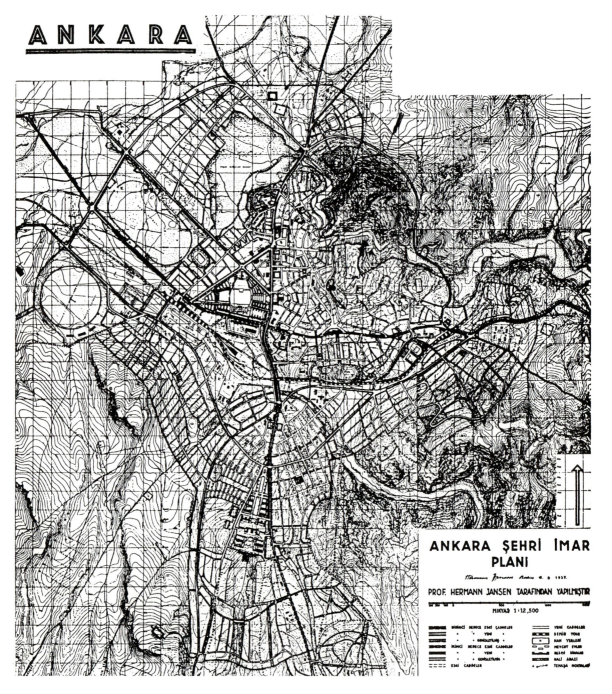

Hermann Jansen. Plan of Ankara. 1932.

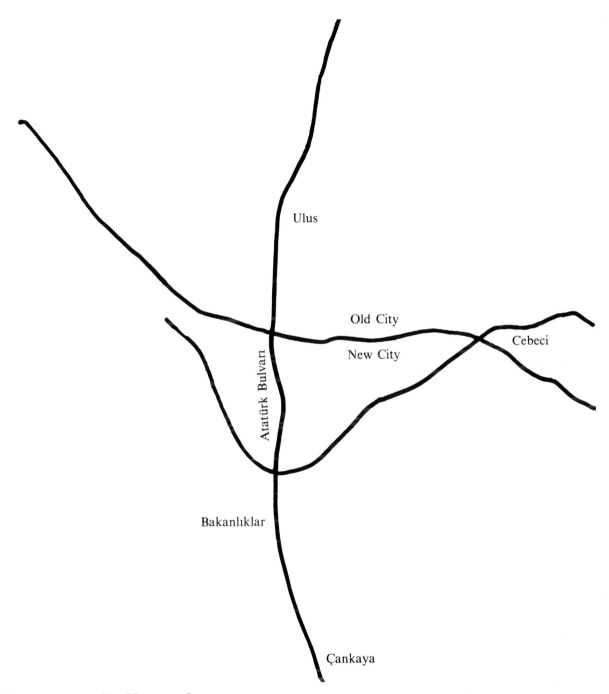

Main axes proposed by Hermann Jansen.

Since then the city expanded towards the south and Çankaya became the upper-income residential area. Yenişehir is the central business district. Administrative center remains in Bakanlıklar, immediately south of which is the Grand National Assembly.

INDEX

LIST OF ILLUSTRATIONS

Fig. 38   Kemalettin Bey, Second Vakıf Apartments, Ankara, 1928. General view from the southwest.

Fig. 39   Mongeri, İş Bankası Headquarters, Ankara, 1928. View of the main entrance facade.

Fig. 40   Mongeri, İş Bankası Headquarters, Ankara, 1928. View of banking hall.

Fig. 41   Mongeri, Agricultural Bank, Ulus, Ankara, 1926-1929. General view.

Fig. 42   Mongeri, Agricultural Bank, Ulus, Ankara, 1926-1929. View of banking hall.

Fig. 43   Mongeri, General Directorate of the State Monopolies (Inhisarlar Idaresi), Ankara, 1928. General view from the northwest.

Fig. 44   Koyunoğlu, Ministry of Foreign Affairs, later Ministry of Customs and State Monopolies, Ankara, 1927. General view from the west.

Fig. 45   Koyunoğlu, Museum of Ethnography, Ankara.

Fig. 46   Koyunoğlu, The Turkish Hearth (Türk Ocağı), Ankara, 1927-1930.

Fig. 47   Kemalettin Bey, Gazi Teachers' College, Ankara, 1926-1930. General view from the southeast.

Fig. 48   Kemalettin Bey, Gazi Teachers' College, Ankara, 1926-1930. Original ground floor plan.

Fig. 49   Kemalettin Bey, Gazi Teachers' College, Ankara, 1926-1930. Auditorium.

Fig. 50   Akalın, Railroad Terminal, Ankara, 1937. Detail of interior.

Fig. 51   Sümerbank Textile Plant, Nazilli, 1935-1937.

Fig. 52   Necmeddin, Gazi Primary School (Gazi Ilk Mektebi), Izmir, 1934.

Fig. 53   Denktaş, Tüten Apartments, Istanbul, 1936.

Fig. 54   Post, Ministry of Health (Sağlık Bakanlığı), Ankara, 1926-1927.

Fig. 55   Holzmeister, Ministry of Defense (Millî Savunma Bakanlığı), Ankara, 1927-1931.

Fig. 56   Holzmeister, General Staff (Genelkurmay Başkanlığı), Ankara, 1929-1930.

Fig. 57   Holzmeister, Ministry of the Interior (İçişleri Bakanlığı), Ankara, 1932-1934.

Fig. 58   Holzmeister, Officers' Club (Orduevi), Ankara, 1929-1933. Main block.

Fig. 59   Holzmeister, The Residence of the President (Cumhurbaşkanlığı Köşkü), Ankara, 1930-1932. General view.

Fig. 60   Holzmeister, The Residence of the President (Cumhurbaşkanlığı Köşkü), Ankara, 1930-1932. Plan of first and second levels.

Fig. 61   Egli, Court of Financial Appeals (Sayıştay), Ankara, 1928-1930.

Fig. 62   Egli, Ismetpaşa Institute for Girls, Ankara, 1930.

Fig. 63   Holtay, Observatory of the University of Istanbul, ıstanbul, 1934-1936.

Fig. 88   Erol, City Hall (Belediye Sarayı), Istanbul, 1953. Its columnar base, its free-form roof structure, its grid facade and recessed windows introduce the International Style into the heart of the old city.

Fig. 89   Tokay and Tayman, Emek Building, Ankara, 1959-1964.

Fig. 90   Çinici, Doruk and Tokay, General Directorate of State Waterworks (Devlet Su İşleri), Ankara, completed 1964.

Fig. 91   Çinici, Doruk and Tokay, General Directorate of State Waterworks (Devlet Su İşleri), Ankara, completed 1964. Ground floor plan.

Fig. 92   Bozkurt, Bolak and Beken, Ulus Center, Ankara, 1954.

Fig. 93   Bozkurt, Bolak and Beken, Ulus Center, Ankara, 1954. A typical office floor plan.

Fig. 94   Devres and Özsan, Etibank Headquarters, Ankara, 1955-1960.

Fig. 95   Devres and Özsan, Etibank Headquarters, Ankara, 1955-1960. Second-level plan.

Fig. 96   Sauger, Grand Hotel (Büyük Ankara), Ankara, 1958-1965.

Fig. 97   Cansever, Karatepe Open Air Museum, Adana.

Fig. 98   Cansever, Karatepe Open Air Museum, Adana. Plan.

Fig. 99   Cansever and Hancı, Anadolu Club, Büyükada, Istanbul, 1959.

Fig. 100   Tekeli, Sisa and Hepgüler, Complex of Retail Shops (Manifaturacılar Çarşısı), Istanbul, 1959.

Fig. 101   Baysal and Birsel, Hukukçular Apartments, Istanbul, 1960-1961.

Fig. 102   Menteşe and Project Office of the Emlâk Kredi Bankası, Ataköy Development, Istanbul, Phase I, 1961.

Fig. 103   Cansever with Yener, Turkish Historical Society (Türk Tarih Kurumu), Ankara, 1966. (Photo: Christopher Little/Aga Khan Award for Architecture)

Fig. 104   Çilingiroğlu and Tunca, Tercüman Newspaper Offices, Istanbul, 1974. Extreme formal disintegration, the abandonment of raw cement and endless articulation of masses.

Fig. 105   Çilingiroğlu and Çinici, Middle East Technical University, Faculty of Architecture, Ankara, 1962-1963. Planned along a central axis, the dynamic new university campus utilizes exposed concrete (*beton brut*) extensively. The Faculty of Architecture displays pavilion-type planning and brings in details of the Japanese interpretation of new Brutalism.

Fig. 106   Bediz and Kamçıl, State Mining Institute (MTA) Buildings, Ankara, early 1960s. This is a transitional building between two periods; it accepts the formal geometric order of the International Style but introduces a new morphic expression.

Fig. 107   Vanlı and Gömleksizoğlu, Ministry of Defense Student Dormitories, Ankara, 1967-1968. Dormitories accommodate students whose parents are Ministry of Defense personnel.

Fig. 108   Çinici and Çinici, Middle East Technical University Auditorium, Ankara.

Fig. 109   Hadi, Hadi and Başçetinçelik, Istanbul University Central Library, Istanbul, 1964-1981.

CONTRIBUTORS

Üstün Alsaç, lecturer in design and modern architecture at Karadeniz Technical University, Trabzon (1969-1980), is now in private practice in Istanbul.

Afife Batur is Associate Professor of Restoration and History of Architecture at Istanbul Technical University.

Ahmet Evin is Assistant Professor of Turkish and Director of the Middle East Center at the University of Pennsylvania.

Renata Holod is Associate Professor of the History of Art and Architecture at the University of Pennsylvania, and has been the Convener of the Aga Khan Award for Architecture.

Yıldız Sey is Professor of Building Systems at the Faculty of Architecture, Istanbul Technical University.

Mete Tapan is Associate Professor of Design at the Faculty of Architecture, Istanbul Technical University.

Ilhan Tekeli is Professor of City and Regional Planning at the Middle East Technical University, Ankara.

Yıldırım Yavuz has taught at the Middle East Technical University and has served as Chairman of the Department of Architecture.

Atilla Yücel is Associate Professor of Theory of Architecture and Architectural Semiology at Istanbul Technical University.

Understanding Stress

Edited by Christina Hughes

Series Editor: Cara Acred

Vol.102

Independence Educational Publishers

First published by Independence

The Studio, High Green, Great Shelford

Cambridge CB22 5EG

England

© Independence 2015

British Library Cataloguing in Publication Data

Understanding stress. -- (Issues today ; 102)

1. Stress (Psychology) 2. Stress management.

I. Series II. Acred, Cara editor.

155.9'042-dc23

ISBN-13: 9781861687234

Acknowledgements

The publisher is grateful for permission to reproduce the material in this book. While every care has been taken to trace and acknowledge copyright, the publisher tenders its apology for any accidental infringement or where copyright has proved untraceable. The publisher would be pleased to come to a suitable arrangement in any such case with the rightful owner.

Illustrations

All illustrations, including the front cover, are by Don Hatcher.

Images

Page 4: © Peter Murphy, page 7: © Claudio Ventrella, page 10: iStock, page 13: SXC, page 23: iStock.

Icons on pages 11, 12 and 15 are courtesy of Freepik.

Editorial by Christina Hughes and layout by Jackie Staines, on behalf of Independence Educational Publishers.

Printed in Great Britain by Zenith Print Group.

Cara Acred

Cambridge

September 2015